D1481529

НАРОДНЫЙ КОМИССАРИАТ ЮСТИЦИИ С.С.С.Р.

СУДЕБНЫЙ ОТЧЕТ

по

ДЕЛУ ТРОЦКИСТСКО-ЗИНОВЬЕВСКОГО ТЕРРОРИСТИЧЕСКОГО ЦЕНТРА

рассмотренному

ВОЕННОЙ КОЛЛЕГИЕЙ ВЕРХОВНОГО СУДА СОЮЗА ССР

19 — 24 августа 1936 г.

ПО ОБВИНЕНИЮ

Зиновьева Г. Е., Каменева Л. Б., Евдокимова Г. Е., Смирнова И. Н., Бакаева И. П., Тер-Ваганяна В. А., Мрачковского С. В., Дрейцера Е. А., Гольцмана Э. С., Рейнгольда И. И., Пикеля Р. В., Ольберга В. П., Бермана-Юрина К. Б., Фрица Давида (Круглянского И. И.), М. Лурье и Н. Лурье

по ст.ст. 58^8, 19 и 58^8, 58^{11}
УК РСФСР

Издание

Народного Комиссариата Юстиции СССР
Москва 1936

REPORT OF COURT PROCEEDINGS

THE CASE OF THE

TROTSKYITE-ZINOVIEVITE TERRORIST CENTRE

Heard Before the

MILITARY COLLEGIUM OF THE
SUPREME COURT OF THE U.S.S.R.

Moscow, August 19-24, 1936

In re

*G. E. Zinoviev, L. B. Kamenev, G. E. Evdokimov,
I. N. Smirnov, I. P. Bakayev, V. A. Ter-Vaganyan,
S. V. Mrachkovsky, E. A. Dreitzer, E. S. Holtzman,
I. I. Reingold, R. V. Pickel, V. P. Olberg, K. B.
Berman-Yurin, Fritz David (I. I. Kruglyansky),
M. Lurye and N. Lurye*

Charged under Articles 58[8], 19 and 58[8], 58[11]
of the Criminal Code of the R.S.F.S.R.

NEW YORK

Howard Fertig

1967

Translated into English from the report
as published in the IZVESTIA TsIK SSSR

First published in 1936 by the
People's Commissariat of Justice of the U.S.S.R.

Howard Fertig, Inc. edition 1967

All rights reserved.

Library of Congress Catalog Card Number: 67-13635

PRINTED IN THE UNITED STATES OF AMERICA
BY NOBLE OFFSET PRINTERS, INC.

CONTENTS

CONTENTS

REPORT OF COURT PROCEEDINGS

AUGUST 19 (MORNING SESSION)

The Court Session of the Military Collegium of the Supreme Court of the U.S.S.R. opens on August 19, 1936 at 12:10 p.m. in the October Hall of the House of Trade Unions. The Court is presided over by Army Military Jurist V. V. Ulrich. Members of the Court: Army Corps Military Jurist I. O. Matulevich and Divisional Military Jurist I. I. Nikitchenko; reserve member of the Court: Divisional Military Jurist I. T. Golyakov; and secretary: Military Jurist of First Rank A. F. Kostyushko.

The prosecution is conducted by Comrade A. Y. Vyshinsky, State Attorney of the U.S.S.R.

The President, Comrade Ulrich, declares the session of the Court open, establishes the identity of the accused, and inquires of them whether they take exception to the composition of the Court or of the State Prosecution. After receiving the reply that there is no such objection, the President announces that all the accused having declined the services of counsel for defence, all rights of the defence are extended to them personally, *i.e.*, the right to put questions to the witnesses and to the other accused, to petition the Court in all matters of procedure, to deliver speeches in their own defence, etc. In addition to this, they retain the right of last pleas.

The Secretary of the Court reads the indictment.

INDICTMENT

in the case of G. E. Zinoviev, L. B. Kamenev, G. E. Evdokimov, I. N. Smirnov, I. P. Bakayev, V. A. Ter-Vaganyan, S. V. Mrachkovsky, E. A. Dreitzer, E. S. Holtzman, I. I. Reingold, R. V. Pickel, V. P. Olberg, K. B. Berman-Yurin, Fritz David (I. I. Kruglyansky), M. Lurye and N. Lurye, accused of crimes covered by Articles 58^8, 19 and 58^8, 58^{11} of the Criminal Code of the R.S.F.S.R.

9

On Jan. 15-16, 1935, the Military Collegium of the Supreme Court of the U.S.S.R. at a special session in the city of Leningrad tried the case of the underground counter-revolutionary group of Zinovievites calling itself the "Moscow centre," the principal leaders of which among the others convicted in that case were *G. E. Zinoviev, L. B. Kamenev, G. E. Evdokimov* and *I. P. Bakayev.*

The preliminary and the Court investigation of that case established that for a number of years this so-called "Moscow centre" guided the counter-revolutionary activities of diverse underground groups of Zinovievites, including the counter-revolutionary activities of the Leningrad group of *Nikolayev-Kotolynov* which on Dec. 1, 1934, foully murdered Comrade *S. M. Kirov.*

The trial established that the so-called "Moscow centre," being the ideological and political leader of the Leningrad group of Zinovievites, knew that this group was inclined towards terrorism and did all it could to fan this inclination.

This had to be admitted also by the accused *Zinoviev* and *Kamenev,* who denied that they took any part in the murder of Comrade *S. M. Kirov,* hypocritically stating at the trial that they bore only moral and political responsibility for the assassination of Comrade *Kirov.*

It now transpires that eighteen months ago, during the investigation of the case of the assassination of Comrade *S. M. Kirov,* the investigating and judicial authorities were not in possession of all the facts revealing the true role of the Zinovievite leaders of the so-called "Moscow centre" on the one hand and the leaders of the Trotskyite underground organization on the other, in the white-guard, terroristic underground activities.

On the strength of newly revealed circumstances ascertained by the investigating authorities in 1936 in connection with the discovery of a number of terrorist groups of Trotskyites and Zinovievites, the investigation has established that *Zinoviev, Kamenev, Evdokimov* and *Bakayev,* who were convicted in the "Moscow centre" case, actually not only knew that their adherents in Leningrad were inclined towards terrorism, but were the direct organizers of the assassination of Comrade *S. M. Kirov.*

The investigation also established that *Zinoviev, Kamenev, Evdokimov, Bakayev,* and a number of other accused in the present case, who will be mentioned later, were the initiators and organizers of attempts which were being prepared on the lives of other leaders of the Communist Party of the Soviet Union and of the Soviet Government as well.

The investigation has also established that the Zinovievites pursued their criminal terroristic practices in a direct *bloc* with the Trotskyites and with *L. Trotsky,* who is abroad.

These newly revealed circumstances establish without a doubt that:

1) At the end of 1932 the Trotskyite and Zinovievite groups united and formed a united centre consisting of *Zinoviev, Kamenev, Evdokimov, Bakayev* (from the Zinovievites) and *I. N. Smirnov, Ter-Vaganyan* and *Mrachkovsky* (from the Trotskyites), all charged in the present case.

2) The principal condition for the union of these counterrevolutionary groups was their common recognition of individual terrorism against the leaders of the C.P.S.U. and the Soviet Government.

3) Precisely from that time onwards (end of 1932) the Trotskyites and Zinovievites, acting on direct instructions from *L. Trotsky,* received by the united centre through special agents, concentrated their hostile activities against the C.P.S.U. and the Soviet Government mainly on the organization of terrorism against the most prominent leaders of the Party and the Government.

4) With this end in view the united centre organized special terrorist groups, which prepared a number of practical measures for the assassination of Comrades *Stalin, Voroshilov, Kaganovich, Kirov, Orjonikidze, Zhdanov, Kossior, Postyshev* and others.

5) One of these terrorist groups, consisting of *Nikolayev, Rumyantsev, Mandelstamm, Levin, Kotolynov* and others, who were convicted by the Military Collegium of the Supreme Court of the U.S.S.R. on Dec. 28-29, 1934, carried out the foul murder of Comrade *S. M. Kirov* on Dec. 1, 1934, on the direct instructions from *Zinoviev* and *L. Trotsky,* and under the direct guidance of the united centre.

11

I. The Trotskyite-Zinovievite United Terrorist Centre

The testimonies of *Zinoviev, Kamenev, Evdokimov, Mrachkov-sky, Bakayev* and a number of other accused in the present case, have established beyond doubt that the only motive for organizing the Trotskyite-Zinovievite *bloc* was their striving to seize power at all costs, and that the sole and decisive means chosen for this purpose was the organization of terroristic acts against the most prominent leaders of the Party and the Government.

Lacking all support in the working class and the toiling masses of the people of the U.S.S.R., having lost all their ideological possessions, having no political program and imbued with bitter hatred toward the Socialist victories of our country, the leaders of the Trotskyite-Zinovievite counter-revolutionary *bloc, Trotsky, Zinoviev* and *Kamenev,* sank definitively into the swamp of white-guardism, joined forces and merged with the most inveterate enemies of the Soviet Power, and became the organizing force of the last remnants of the exploiting classes which had been routed in the U.S.S.R. In their desperation and hatred they resorted to the most despicable means of fighting the Soviet Government and the leaders of the C.P.S.U., namely, political assassinations.

At first, in the face of the first successes of Socialism in the U.S.S.R., they held to their hopes that difficulties would arise, with which, in their calculations, the Soviet Power would not be able to cope. But later, seeing that these difficulties were being successfully overcome and that our country was emerging victorious from these difficulties, they frankly banked on the complication of international relations, on war and the defeat of the Soviet Power.

Seeing no favourable prospects for themselves, they resorted to the gun; they organized underground terroristic groups and made use of the most detestable method of fighting, namely terrorism.

At present the Trotskyite-Zinovievite conspirators, as a reason for their fight against the C.P.S.U. and the Soviet Government, no longer advance the claim that the Party and the Soviet Government are pursuing an allegedly wrong policy, or that the C.P.S.U. and the Soviet Government are leading the country to its doom, as they lyingly and slanderously asserted in the past. As their principal motive for resorting to terrorism they now advance the successes of the building of Socialism in the U.S.S.R., the successes in the cultural and economic growth of the country, which successes, demonstrating the ideological and political bankruptcy of the Trotskyites-Zinovievites, fan their hatred of the Soviet Government still more and intensify their desire to avenge themselves on the Soviet Government for their political failure by resorting to terrorism.

In spite of obdurate denials, the accused *Zinoviev* was compelled by the weight of evidence which was laid before him by the investigating authorities to admit that:

"... The main object which the Trotskyite-Zinovievite centre pursued was the assassination of the leaders of the C.P.S.U., and in the first place the assassination of *Stalin* and *Kirov*." (Vol. XII, p. 16.)

Another member of this centre, the accused *Reingold,* during examination on July 3, 1936, testified:

"... The main thing on which all the members of the *bloc* agreed was ... the recognition of the necessity of consolidating all forces to capture the Party leadership. I must admit that the fundamental aim of the Trotskyite-Zinovievite *bloc* was to remove by violence the leadership of the C.P.S.U. and the Soviet Government, and *Stalin* in the first place. At the end of 1932 the centre adopted a decision to organize the fight against the leadership of the C.P.S.U. and the Government by terroristic means. I know that the Trotskyite section of the *bloc* received instructions from *L. D. Trotsky* to adopt the path of terrorism and to prepare attempts on the life of *Stalin*." (Vol. XXVII, p. 52.)

Exhaustive evidence on the same point was also given during the examination on July 23, 1936 by the accused *Kamenev*. The accused *Kamenev* stated:

"... The emergence from the difficulties, the victory of the policy of the Central Committee of the C.P.S.U. caused in us a new wave of animosity and hatred towards the leadership of the Party, and primarily towards *Stalin*."

"... We, *i.e.*, the Zinovievite centre of the counter-revolutionary organization, the members of which I have enumerated above, and the Trotskyite counter-revolutionary organization in the persons of *Smirnov, Mrachkovsky* and *Ter-Vaganyan,* negotiated in 1932 to unite both the Zinovievite and Trotskyite counter-revolutionary organizations for joint preparation of terroristic acts against the leaders of the Central Committee and in the first place against *Stalin* and *Kirov.*"

"... The main thing is that in 1932 both *Zinoviev* and we, namely, myself *(Kamenev), Evdokimov, Bakayev* and the Trotskyite leaders, *Smirnov, Mrachkovsky* and *Ter-Vaganyan,* decided that the only means by which we could hope to come to power was to organize terroristic acts against the leaders of the C.P.S.U., and primarily against *Stalin.* It was precisely on this basis of a terroristic struggle against the leaders of the C.P.S.U. that negotiations for the union were conducted between ourselves and the Trotskyites."

(Vol. XV, pp. 10, 12, 13.)

The accused *Kamenev* further stated that:

"... However, our banking on the insuperability of the difficulties which the country was experiencing, on the state of crisis of its economy, on the collapse of the economic policy of the Party leadership had obviously failed by the second half of 1932.

"Overcoming the difficulties, the country, under the leadership of the Central Committee of the C.P.S.U., was successfully advancing along the road of economic growth. We could not help seeing this.

"One would have thought that we should have stopped fighting. But the logic of the counter-revolutionary struggle, the nakedly unprincipled striving to seize power led us in the other direction. The emergence from the difficulties, the victory of the policy of the Central Committee of the C.P.S.U., caused in us a new wave of animosity and hatred towards the leaders of the Party, and primarily towards *Stalin.*"

(Vol. XV, p. 27.)

14

This was confirmed also by the accused *Evdokimov* who, on Aug. 10 this year, gave detailed evidence on the organization of the united centre and the terroristic position adopted by it. In reply to the question put to him by the investigating authorities on what basis the Trotskyite-Zinovievite *bloc* arose, the accused *Evdokimov* stated:

". . . *Mrachkovsky* said: 'The hopes we have placed on the collapse of the Party's policy must be considered doomed. The methods of struggle used up to now have not produced any positive results. There remains only one path of struggle, and that is the removal of the leadership of the Party and the Government by violence . . .' Seeing that I agreed with him, *Mrachkovsky*, no longer having any fear that I would not support him, went on to say: '*Stalin* and the other leaders of the Party and the Government must be removed. This is the principal task.'

"Right there, *Mrachkovsky* informed me that the Trotskyites had received instructions from *Trotsky* on the necessity of organizing terroristic attempts on the lives of the leaders of the Party and the Government, that *Trotsky*, being outside the Soviet Union, correctly defined the tasks of the fight against the leadership of the C.P.S.U. At the same time, by the logic of the struggle, *Mrachkovsky* himself and other Trotskyites had come to the conclusion that terrorism was the only road of struggle remaining. . . . *Smirnov* expressed the same views as *Mrachkovsky*. . . . In conclusion *Mrachkovsky* and *Smirnov* proposed to unite the forces of the Trotskyites and Zinovievites and to proceed to create secret terrorist groups for the purpose of committing terroristic acts against the leaders of the Party and the Government.

(Vol. XXXVI, p. 10.)

Similar evidence was also given by a member of the Moscow terrorist centre, *I. I. Reingold,* who testified as follows:

". . . I met *Kamenev* in the second half of 1933 and also in 1934 in his apartment in Karmanitsky pereulok, in Moscow.

Kamenev appraised the situation in approximately the same way as *Zinoviev* and backed his conclusions by an analysis of the economic and political situation in the country *Kamenev* arrived at the conclusion that after all, things were not moving toward catastrophe but were on the up-grade; therefore, all expectations of an automatic collapse were groundless, and the leadership that had grown up was made of too hard a granite to expect that it would split of itself. From this *Kamenev* drew the conclusion that the 'leadership will have to be split.'

"Kamenev repeatedly quoted *Trotsky* as saying: 'the whole matter is in the top, therefore the top must be removed.'

"*Kamenev* advocated the necessity of a terrorist struggle and primarily the necessity of killing *Stalin,* pointing out that this was the only way of coming to power. I particularly remember his cynical remark that 'heads are peculiar in that they do not grow on again.'

"*Kamenev* proposed that terrorist gunmen be trained. He said that the distinguishing feature of the new *bloc* compared with the previous opposition *bloc* was the adoption of energetic terroristic action."   (Vol. XXVII, p. 61.)

He further said:

". . . I have already stated above that the Trotskyite-Zinovievite united *bloc* had no new political program. It based itself upon the old threadbare platform, and none of the leaders of the *bloc* occupied themselves with, or were interested in the question of drawing up any kind of political program that was to any degree complete and consistent. The only thing that united this heterogeneous *bloc* was the idea of a terrorist fight against the leaders of the Party and the Government.

"As a matter of fact the *bloc* was a counter-revolutionary terrorist gang of assassins who strove to seize power in the country by any means whatever."

(Vol. XXVII, pp. 72-73.)

16

The accused *I. N. Smirnov,* during examination on Aug. 5, 1936, also admitted that he had met *Sedov, L. Trotsky's* son, while he was in Berlin as far back as 1931.

I. N. Smirnov stated:

"... In the course of our conversation, *L. Sedov,* analysing the situation in the Soviet Union, expressed the opinion that under the present conditions only the removal by violence of the leading persons in the C.P.S.U. and the Soviet Government could bring about a change in the general situation in the country...."

"... I admit that the attitude which regarded terrorism as the only way of changing the situation in the Soviet Union was known to me from a conversation with *Sedov* in Berlin in 1931 as his own personal position. I admit that this line on terrorism was confirmed by *L. Trotsky* in 1932 in his personal instructions conveyed to me through *Y. Gaven.*

"I admit that *Ter-Vaganyan,* who with my knowledge conducted negotiations with the Leftists and the Zinovievites in the name of the Trotskyite group, formed in 1932 a *bloc* with *Kamenev, Zinoviev* and the *Lominadze* group for joint strug· gle against the C.P.S.U. and the Soviet Government, and that *L. Trotsky's* instructions regarding terror against the leaders of the C.P.S.U. and the Soviet state were made the basis of this *bloc.*" (Vol. XXIX, pp. 93, 104.)

The accused *V. A. Ter-Vaganyan* confirmed this evidence of the accused *Smirnov,* admitting his participation in the united centre, as well as the participation in this centre of the accused *I. N. Smirnov, Mrachkovsky, Zinoviev* and *Kamenev.*

The accused *Ter-Vaganyan* admitted that:

"The Trotskyite organization headed by *I. N Smirnov,* in its counter-revolutionary activities, particularly fostered hatred and animosity against the leaders of the C.P.S.U. . . . It was on this hatred that the *bloc* was founded. . . ."
(Vol. XXXVIII, p. 11.)

The accused *Ter-Vaganyan* also admitted that as far back as 1931—

"*Sedov* received from *Trotsky* special instructions for *I. N. Smirnov* and the underground Trotskyites in the U.S.S.R. to adopt the most active and sharp methods of struggle against the Party and its leadership."

(Vol. XXXVIII, p. 27.)

Confirming the evidence of the accused *Mrachkovsky* on this point, the accused *Ter-Vaganyan* testified:

"*Mrachkovsky* is right when he says that the Trotskyite-Zinovievite *bloc* itself was really organized on the basis of the recognition that it was necessary to fight the leadership of the Party and the Government by terroristic methods."

(Vol. XXXVIII, p. 32.)

Thus, there is no doubt left that the Trotskyite-Zinovievite *bloc* had turned into a group of unprincipled, political adventurers and assassins striving at only one thing, namely, to make their way to power even through terrorism.

Such is the sole and exhaustive "program" of this association of political assassins.

Concerning terrorism as the sole basis on which the union of the Trotskyites and Zinovievites took place in 1932, evidence was given at the preliminary investigation also by the accused *R. V. Pickel*. During the examination on July 23, *Pickel* testified:

". . . According to the information conveyed to us by *Reingold* in the beginning of 1934, the all-Union united counter-revolutionary centre of the Trotskyite-Zinovievite *bloc* decided by the efforts of the Trotskyites and Zinovievites to strike a crushing blow at the C.P.S.U. by committing a number of terroristic acts with the aim of beheading the leadership and seizing power.

"The all-Union centre of the Trotskyite-Zinovievite *bloc* then bluntly raised the question of the necessity of 'surgical intervention' (meaning terrorism) in order to bring about a decisive change in the situation in the country. For this purpose the centre gave instructions to start selecting people who nursed particularly bitter feelings against the Party leadership, who had very strong will power and were capable

18

of carrying out terroristic attempts on the lives of the leaders of the C.P.S.U." (Vol. XXV, p. 65.)

In conformity with the course taken by the Trotskyite-Zinovievite underground *bloc* of seizing power by any means, the members of this *bloc* widely practised double-dealing as the special and main method in their relations towards the Party and the Government. They brought this double-dealing to monstrous dimensions, and transformed it into a system that might rouse the envy of any Azef and Malinovsky, of any secret service with all its spies, provocateurs and agents for diversive activities.

One of the principal aims of the Trotskyite-Zinovievite *bloc* was in every possible way to conceal and mask its counter-revolutionary activities and the organization of terroristic acts.

On this point the accused *Reingold* testified:

"... In 1933-34 *Zinoviev* told me when I was alone with him in his apartment that: '... The principal practical task is to organize the terroristic work so secretly as to preclude our being compromised in any way....'

"'... When under examination the main thing is persistently to deny any connection with the organization. If accused of terroristic activities, you must emphatically deny it and argue that terror is incompatible with the views of Bolsheviks-Marxists.'" (Vol. XXVII, pp. 110, 112.)

Similar instructions were given by *L. Trotsky*, who recommended that when terroristic acts were committed they should be disavowed and "a position should be taken up analogous to that taken up by the Central Committee of the Socialist-Revolutionaries toward Madame Kaplan" who shot at V. I. Lenin.

Another reason why the united centre resorted to profound secrecy and carefully masked its terroristic activities was that one of its aims was to betray the vigilance of the working class and the masses of the toilers. While preparing the assassination of Comrade *Stalin* and other leaders of the C.P.S.U., the united centre simultaneously strove by all means in its power to give assurances of its loyalty and even devotion to the Party and the Soviet Power, of its repentance of past mistakes and of its readiness to serve

19

the Proletarian Revolution honestly. The leaders of the united centre figured that having been "forgiven" they could, after killing Comrade *Stalin,* utilize this "forgiveness" to come into power. On this point the accused *Reingold* testified:

> ". . . They believed—I am speaking of the leaders of the Trotskyite-Zinovievite centre—that the fact that we were forgiven while *Stalin* was still alive, the fact that confidence was placed in us, would ensure our coming nearer to the leadership and to power; and following this, after *Zinoviev, Kamenev* and their supporters had come into power, they would ensure the return also of *Trotsky* to the leadership and to power."   (Vol. XXVII, p. 168.)

This was also testified to during examination by the accused *Kamenev:*

> "...We discussed this question.more than once. We outlined and decided on two possible ways for the leaders of the Trotskyite-Zinovievite *bloc* to come to power.
>
> "The first, and what seemed to us to be the most feasible way, was that after a terroristic act had been committed against *Stalin,* there would ensue confusion in the leadership of the Party and the Government, and negotiations would be opened with us, the leaders of the Zinovievite *bloc* and in the first place with *Zinoviev, Kamenev* and *Trotsky.*
>
> "We assumed that in these negotiations, myself and *Zinoviev* would occupy the leading positions in the Party and the country, for even with *Stalin* we, by our policy of double-dealing, had obtained, after all, forgiveness of our mistakes by the Party and had been taken back into its ranks, while our participation, that is mine, *Zinoviev's* and *Trotsky's,* in the terroristic acts would remain secret from the Party and the country.
>
> "The second way by which we could seize power, and which seemed to us to be less reliable, was that after a terroristic act had been committed against *Stalin,* the leadership of the Party and the country would be thrown into a state of uncertainty and disorganization.

"The leaders of the Trotskyite-Zinovievite *bloc* would be able to take advantage of the confusion to compel the remaining leaders of the Party to admit us to power or else to yield to us their places.

"*Trotsky's* appearance and his active participation in the struggle for power were taken as a matter of course."

(Vol. XV, pp. 33-34.)

The united Trotskyite-Zinovievite centre took the path of terrorism under the direct influence of *L. D. Trotsky,* who personally gave the members of the united centre a number of verbal and written instructions to this effect.

During examination on July 20, 1936 the accused *S. V. Mrachkovsky* testified:

". . . We Trotskyites adopted the policy of terrorism long before the *bloc* with *Zinoviev* and *Kamenev* was formed. In 1931, when *I. N. Smirnov* was in Berlin and established contact with *L. Trotsky,* instructions were received from the latter to proceed to the organization of action groups of Trotskyites." (Vol. XVIII, pp. 40, 41.)

This same *Mrachkovsky* stated:

". . . According to the instructions of *L. Trotsky* received in 1931 by *I. N. Smirnov,* we were to kill *Stalin, Voroshilov* and *Kaganovich. Stalin* was to be killed first."

(Vol. XVIII, p. 42.)

On *Trotsky's* attitude towards forming, a united Trotskyite-Zinovievite *bloc* and adopting terroristic methods of struggle, the accused *Mrachkovsky* testified as follows:

". . . In the middle of 1932, *I. N. Smirnov* put before our leading trio the question of the necessity of uniting our organization with the *Zinoviev-Kamenev* and *Shatskin-Lominadze* groups . . . It was then decided to consult *L. Trotsky* on this question and to obtain his directions. *L. Trotsky* replied, agreeing to the formation of a *bloc* on the condition that the groups uniting in the *bloc* would agree to the necessity of

21

removing by violence the leaders of the C.P.S.U. and *Stalin* in the first place." (Vol. XVIII, pp. 44, 45.)

This evidence of *Mrachkovsky* was fully confirmed by the accused *Dreitzer* who during examination testified:

"... On the direct instructions of *L. Trotsky,* our all-Union centre of the Trotskyite-Zinovievite *bloc* was to prepare and carry out the assassination of *Stalin* and *Voroshilov* for the purpose of beheading the leadership of the C.P.S.U. and the Red Army." (Vol. X, p. 99.)

In 1934, the accused *Dreitzer* personally received written instructions from *Trotsky,* through *L. Trotsky's* son, *Sedov,* to prepare and carry out a terroristic act against Comrade *Stalin.* This letter was written personally by *Trotsky.* According to *Dreitzer's* testimony the contents of this letter were as follows:

"Dear friend. Convey that today we have the following main tasks before us:
"1) To remove *Stalin* and *Voroshilov.*
"2) To unfold work for organizing nuclei in the army.
"3) In the event of war, to take advantage of every setback and confusion to capture the leadership."

The accused *Dreitzer* stated that "the letter ended with instructions to keep *Trotsky* informed of the progress of the work done in fulfilment of the above instructions. I must add that these instructions of *Trotsky* fully confirmed the instructions I received from *Mrachkovsky* in May 1934." (Vol. X, pp. 102, 103.)

This letter was addressed by *Trotsky* to *Dreitzer* personally as to one of the people most devoted to him, and who at one time was chief of his personal bodyguard.

Dreitzer handed this letter to *Mrachkovsky,* who, according to the testimony of *Dreitzer* and of *Mrachkovsky* himself, eventually destroyed it for reasons of secrecy.

In addition to the above-mentioned letter, *Trotsky* sent to the Trotskyite-Zinovievite centre a number of other verbal and written instructions concerning terrorism. In particular, he handed to the accused *Holtzman* instructions of this nature when he met him personally. *Holtzman,* served as a *liaison* man between *L. Trotsky* and the Trotskyite-Zinovievite centre.

The investigation has established that after the smash-up of the Trotskyite-Zinovievite centre in connection with the murder of Comrade *Kirov, L. Trotsky* himself assumed the leadership of terroristic activities in the U.S.S.R. and began strongly to press forward the organization of the assassinations of Comrades *Stalin* and *Voroshilov.* For this purpose he took steps to restore the terrorist groups in the U.S.S.R. and to stimulate their activity by sending a number of his tried agents to the U.S.S.R. from abroad and also by using for this purpose persons belonging to underground Trotskyite organizations in the U.S.S.R. who went abroad ostensibly on official business.

The investigation has established that at various times the following accused persons were sent from Berlin to Moscow as such agents: *V. Olberg, Berman-Yurin, Fritz David (Kruglyansky), Moissei Lurye, Nathan Lurye* and several others who received directly from *L. D. Trotsky* and his son *Sedov (L. L. Trotsky)* instructions to organize at all costs the assassinations of Comrades *Stalin, Voroshilov, Kaganovich* and other leaders of the Party.

One of these Trotskyite agents, *V. Olberg,* who arrived in the U.S.S.R. with the passport of a citizen of the Republic of Honduras, stated when arrested and examined:

> "... As I have already testified, I began active Trotskyite work at the beginning of 1930. In addition to the persons I have enumerated, I was personally connected with *Trotsky* and his son *Lev Sedov;* I carried out a number of assignments given to me personally by *Trotsky* in connection with the Trotskyite organization, and I was his emissary in Germany. As *Trotsky's* emissary in Germany, I carried on work in the Trotskyite organization in Berlin and also maintained secret connections with the Soviet Union. I maintained connections with the Soviet Union using addresses and places which *Lev Sedov* indicated to me." (Vol. XXI, p. 24.)

V. Olberg admitted that he arrived in the U.S.S.R. illegally for the purpose of carrying on Trotskyite counter-revolutionary work and of organizing a terroristic act against Comrade *Stalin*.

During examination on February 21 of this year, *V. Olberg* testified that during one of his meetings with *L. Trotsky's* son, *Sedov*, the latter showed him a letter from *Trotsky* in which *Trotsky* proposed that *Olberg* be sent to the Soviet Union with a group of German Trotskyites for the purpose of preparing and organizing the murder of *Stalin*.

> "... In this letter," *V. Olberg* goes on to say, "*Trotsky* wrote to *Sedov* stating that he fully agreed with his proposal that I be sent to the Soviet Union. *Trotsky* wrote that he considered me to be an absolutely suitable person who could be fully relied upon in so perilous a matter."

To this *Olberg* added:

> "*Sedov* said to me that it was my duty to conceal by every possible means *Trotsky's* role in the organization of a terroristic act against *Stalin,* and that even if I were arrested in circumstances in which my role of a terrorist would be absolutely obvious, I was to conceal the fact that I was a Trotskyite and was committing the terroristic act on *Trotsky's* instructions." (Vol. XXI, pp. 77, 78.)

As the investigation has established, *V. Olberg* arrived in the U.S.S.R. with the passport of a citizen of the Republic of Honduras obtained with the aid of the German Secret Police (Gestapo).

On this point *V. Olberg,* during examination in the office of the State Attorney of the U.S.S.R., testified

> "... *Sedov* promised to help me to obtain a passport to return to the U.S.S.R. once more. But I succeeded in obtaining a passport with the help of my younger brother, *Paul Olberg*. Thanks to my connections with the German police and their agent in Prague, *V. P. Tukalevsky,* I, by means of a bribe, obtained the passport of a citizen of the Republic of Honduras. The money for the passport—13,000 Czechoslovakian kronen—I obtained from *Sedov,* or rather, from the Trotskyite organization on *Sedov's* instructions." (Vol. XXI, p. 262.)

Re-examined on the question of his connection with the Gestapo, *V. Olberg* on July 31 of this year testified:

> "Confirming also my testimony of May 9 of this year, I emphasize that my connection with the Gestapo was not at all an exception, of which one could speak as of the fall of an individual Trotskyite. It was the line of the Trotskyites in conformity with the instructions of *L. Trotsky* given through *Sedov*. The connection with the Gestapo followed the line of organizing terrorism in the U.S.S.R. against the leaders of the C.P.S.U. and the Soviet Government."
>
> "... Several times I met a prominent official of the Gestapo, whose name was not mentioned to me, and I did not consider it convenient to inquire. With this official I discussed my first journey to Moscow and my plans concerning the preparation of a terroristic act. This official knew my brother as an agent of the Gestapo to whom he advised me to apply for help whenever necessary."
>
> (Vol. XXI, pp. 263-264.)

This testimony of *V. Olberg* was fully confirmed by *Paul Olberg,* also an agent of the German Secret Police, arrested in connection with another case. It was *Paul Olberg* who put his brother *V. Olberg,* as both of them testify, in touch with the Gestapo and helped *V. Olberg* to obtain from the Gestapo the passport of a citizen of the Republic of Honduras, which figures as an exhibit in the present case.

Paul Olberg also confirmed the fact that *V. Olberg's* journey to the U.S.S.R. was organized with terroristic purposes. During examination on May 16 this year, *Paul Olberg* testified:

> "... *Valentine Olberg* informed me that an official of the German Secret Police told him that all persons taking part in preparing and committing terroristic acts would be given refuge in Germany." (Vol. XXIV, p. 231.)

Another Trotskyite agent, sent to the U.S.S.R. with terroristic tasks, namely *Berman-Yurin,* testified:

"... My own role was that I arrived in the U.S.S.R. as a person particularly trusted by *Lev Davidovich Trotsky* with a special mission and instructions from him."

(Vol. IV, p. 30.)

As the investigation has established, this "special mission and instructions" were to organize the assassination of Comrade *Stalin*. This was admitted by the accused *Berman-Yurin,* who testified that, on meeting *L. Trotsky* in Copenhagen, he received from Trotsky directions to kill Comrade *Stalin*.

"... During this conversation," said the accused *Berman-Yurin*, "*Trotsky* openly said to me that in the fight against *Stalin*, one must not hesitate to resort to extreme measures, and that *Stalin* must be physically destroyed."

(Vol. IV, p. 36.)

"... *Trotsky* emphasized that the attempt must be prepared very carefully and circumspectly and should be timed with some big political event of international importance. It would be most preferable, if the opportunity arose, to make the attempt coincide with some plenum or the congress of the Comintern. *Trotsky* stated that such a terroristic act committed at a congress or plenum would immediately assume the nature of an international political event; it would rouse the masses far beyond the frontiers of the U.S.S.R. and would give rise to a powerful movement.

"*Trotsky* told me that this terroristic act against *Stalin* must not be committed secretly, on the quiet, but that the assassination must be committed publicly, before an international forum." (Vol. IV, pp. 38, 39.)

Simultaneously with *Berman-Yurin, L. Trotsky* sent also the accused *Fritz David (I. I. Kruglyansky)* to the U.S.S.R. to prepare terroristic acts.

In the autumn of 1932, *Fritz David (I. I. Kruglyansky)* also had a meeting with *L. Trotsky,* arranged for him by *Sedov*. In conversation with him, *Trotsky* proposed that *Fritz David (I. I. Kruglyansky)* undertake, as he expressed it, the "historic mission" of killing *Stalin*.

26

Fritz David (I. I. Kruglyansky) testified:

"... When proposing that I go to the U.S.S.R. to kill *Stalin,* *Trotsky* advised me, for the sake of secrecy, not to maintain open connections with the Trotskyites but outwardly to adhere to the policy of the Central Committee of the Communist Party of Germany.

"This conversation with *Trotsky* took place in November 1932 and I accepted his proposal to kill *Stalin.*"

(Vol. VIII, p. 73.)

On arriving in the U.S.S.R. *Berman-Yurin* found *Fritz David (I. I. Kruglyansky)* at an address given him by *Sedov. Fritz David (I. I. Kruglyansky)* and *Berman-Yurin* decided to carry out the assassination of Comrade *Stalin* at the Seventh Congress of the Comintern. This, however, they failed to do owing to the fact that *Berman-Yurin* was unable to get into the Congress, while *Fritz David (I. I. Kruglyansky),* although he got into the Congress, could not carry out his criminal intention because he sat far away from the presidium and had no opportunity of getting near to Comrade *Stalin.*

As both of the accused admitted during the investigation, *Fritz David (I. I. Kruglyansky)* was to have shot Comrade *Stalin* at the Seventh Congress with a Browning pistol which he had received from *Berman-Yurin.*   (Vol. VIII, p. 77.)

The investigation has also established that the terrorist group headed by *Trotsky's* agent, *Moissei Lurye,* whom *Trotsky* sent into the U.S.S.R. from abroad, was actually organized by the active German fascist *Franz Weitz,* the representative of Himmler, at that time the leader of the fascist SS Detachments and now the director of the German Secret Police (Gestapo).

On this point *M. Lurye,* examined on July 21, stated:

"*Nathan Lurye* replied that he was still, as before, a convinced Trotskyite, and he reported that a terrorist group, small in number, but very reliable, had been organized here in Moscow in April 1932. . . .

27

"... When I asked on whose instructions and at whose initiative this action group had been organized, *N. Lurye* answered that the action group was created by a certain *Franz Weitz...*"

"... When I asked who was *Franz Weitz, N. Lurye,* at first very unwillingly, answered as follows: *Franz Weitz* is an active member of the National-Socialist Party in Germany and a trusted man of *Himmler* (the present director of the Gestapo in Germany). At that time *Himmler* was the leader of the 'SS'—Blackshirt Guards..."

"... The main task of the group, according to *Weitz,* was to prepare terroristic acts against *Stalin, Kaganovich, Voroshilov and Orjonikidze...*" (Vol. XXXII, pp. 243, 244.)

The accused *M. Lurye* communicated to Zinoviev in detail *N. Lurye's* report, desiring to ascertain *Zinoviev's* attitude towards connections with the fascists and the German Secret Police.

After listening to *M. Lurye's* communication, *Zinoviev* replied:

"What is there in this to disturb you? You are a historian, *Moissei Ilyich,* you know the case of Lassalle and Bismarck, when Lassalle wanted to use Bismarck in the interests of the revolution."

"... By means of this historical parallel," added *M. Lurye,* "*Zinoviev* wanted to prove the possibility and the necessity of utilizing an alliance with the National-Socialists in the fight against the C.P.S.U. and the Soviet Government."

(Vol. XXXII, p. 252.)

M. Lurye's testimony was fully confirmed by *N. Lurye,* who, during examination on July 21 testified as follows:

"I must admit that from the autumn of 1932 to the end of 1933 the terrorist action group of which I was the head, was actively preparing a terroristic act against the People's Commissar of Defence, *Voroshilov....*"

"... I was commissioned to do this by *Franz Weitz,* a German engineer-architect, member of the National-Socialist

Party of Germany, representative of *Himmler,* now director of the Gestapo."

"... In August 1932, leaving for Germany for his vacation, *Franz Weitz* put me in charge of the terrorist action group and set before me the task of preparing and carrying out ter- roristic acts against *Stalin, Kaganovich* and *Voroshilov."*

(Vol. XXXIII, pp. 141-142.)

Thus the accused *M. Lurye* and *N. Lurye,* by establishing direct organizational contact with the German fascists and the Ger- man Secret Police, betrayed the interests of the Soviet State and committed treason against their country.

Finally, the circumstances established by the investigation show that *L. Trotsky, Zinoviev, Kamenev* and others, the leaders of the Trotskyite-Zinovievite *bloc,* in their fight against the Soviet Government sank so low that their morals proved to be more con- temptible than those of gangs of the most hardened criminals. While organizing terroristic acts against the leaders of the C.P.S.U. and the Soviet State, the leaders of the united centre simulta- neously were preparing to exterminate their own terrorist agents, in order completely to wipe out all traces of their crimes.

On this point the accused *Reingold* testified as follows:

"Zinoviev and *Kamenev* did not exclude the possibility that the O.G.P.U. was in possession of the threads of the con- spiracy against the State which was being prepared by them. Therefore they regarded it as their most important task to destroy every possible trace of the crimes committed. For this purpose it was proposed to appoint *Bakayev* chairman of the O.G.P.U. He was to be charged with the function of physically exterminating the persons who directly carried out terroristic acts against *Stalin* and *Kirov,* as well as those workers of the O.G.P.U. who might be in possession of the threads of the crimes committed."

(Vol. XXVII, pp. 163-164.)

II. *The United Trotskyite-Zinovievite Centre and the Assassination of Comrade S. M. Kirov*

It was already established in the case of *Nikolayev, Rumyantsev, Kotolynov* and others shot by sentence of the Military Collegium of the Supreme Court of the U.S.S.R. on the charge of murdering Comrade *S. M. Kirov* on December 1, 1934, that direct connections existed between the group of Zinovievites in Leningrad who committed the murder, and the accused *Zinoviev, Kamenev* and *Bakayev,* already convicted in the case of the so-called "Moscow centre."

At the present time, the investigating authorities are in possession of facts establishing beyond doubt that the murder of *S. M. Kirov* was committed in accordance with the decision of the united Trotskyite-Zinovievite centre.

This was admitted at the preliminary investigation by the majority of active members of various terrorist Trotskyite-Zinovievite groups, including the accused *Zinoviev, Kamenev, Evdokimov, Bakayev, Mrachkovsky* and others.

The accused *Evdokimov* fully confirmed this by declaring at the examination on Aug. 10 of this year the following:

"... At the trial of the Kirov murder case, I—*Evdokimov,* with *Zinoviev, Kamenev, Bakayev, Gertik* and others, deceived the Government authorities and the Court by concealing that the murder of Kirov was prepared and carried out by us, the members of the Trotskyite-Zinovievite *bloc.*

"The murder of Kirov was committed by the Leningrad terrorist centre on the direct instructions of the united centre of the Trotskyite-Zinovievite *bloc.* (Vol. XXXVI, p. 6.)

"... In 1934, *Zinoviev,* acting in the name of the Trotskyite-Zinovievite organization, gave *Bakayev* direct instructions to organize the murder of Kirov.

In addition to *Zinoziev* those taking part in the decision to murder *Kirov,* included *Kamenev,* myself—*Evdokimov, Bakayev,* and also representatives of the Trotskyites in the persons of *Mrachkovsky* and *Ter-Vaganyan.* In order to prepare the murder, *Bakayev* went to Leningrad in the autumn of 1934 and there established contact with the active members of our organization: *Kotolynov, Levin, Rumyantsev, Mandelstamm* and *Myasnikov*, who formed the so-called Leningrad terrorist centre. The Leningrad centre had an active group of terrorists, directly engaged in preparations for the murder of *Kirov*." (Vol. XXXVI, p. 6.)

After obdurate denials, the accused *Zinoviev*, convicted by the testimony of a number of other accused, had to admit that as far back as 1932 the united Trotskyite-Zinovievite centre had decided to organize terroristic acts against Comrade *Stalin* in Moscow and against Comrade *Kirov* in Leningrad.

"In the autumn of 1932," stated the accused *Zinoviev*, "in my villa at Ilyinskoye, in the presence of *Kamenev, Bakayev, Evdokimov* and *Karev*, I instructed *Bakayev* to prepare a terroristic act against *Stalin*, and *Karev* to prepare a terroristic act against *Kirov*." (Vol. XII p. 36.)

The accused *Zinoviev* testified:

"In 1934, I do not remember the exact month, in the middle of the year, *Evdokimov* informed me of one of *Gertik's* trips to Leningrad during which *Gertik* established contact with *Kotolynov*. As a result of this meeting *Kotolynov* told *Gertik* that he was taking a direct part in the preparations for the assassination of *Kirov*." (Vol. XII, pp. 37, 38.)

This was also testified by the accused *Kamenev*, who confirmed the fact that a conference had taken place in Ilyinskoye at which it was decided to commit terroristic acts against Comrades *Stalin* and *Kirov*. The accused *Kamenev* testified:

"I must admit that before the conference in Ilyinskoye, *Zinoviev* informed me of the proposed decisions of the centre of the Trotskyite-Zinovievite *bloc* to organize terroristic acts against *Stalin* and *Kirov*, declaring that the representatives of the Trotskyites in the centre of the *bloc, Smirnov, Mrachkovsky* and *Ter-Vaganyan*, emphatically insisted on this decision, that they had direct instructions on this matter from

31

Trotsky, and that they demanded that a start be made in putting these measures into practice in pursuance of those principles which formed the basis of the *bloc."*

(Vol. XV, pp. 15, 16.)

To this the accused *Kamenev* added:

"I joined in this decision being in full agreement with it."

(Vol. XV, p. 16.)

As the investigation has established, the practical fulfilment of the plan to organize the murder of Comrade *Kirov* was assigned by the united centre to *I. P. Bakayev,* a member of that centre.

Direct evidence on this is given by the accused *Zinoviev,* who admitted that it was precisely *Bakayev* who had been instructed by *Zinoviev,* in the name of the united centre, to organize the terroristic acts against Comrade *Stalin* in Moscow and against Comrade *Kirov* in Leningrad. (Vol. XII, p. 36.)

Detailed evidence on the role played by *Zinoviev, Bakayev* and the whole of the united Trotskyite-Zinovievite centre in the murder of Comrade *S. M. Kirov* was given by the accused *Reingold,* who stated the following:

"I learned personally from *Zinoviev* that the assassination of *Kirov* in Leningrad was prepared on his direct instructions and on the instructions of the centre of the Trotskyite-Zinovievite *bloc.* During this conversation with *Zinoviev,* which took place in his apartment in August 1934, he, as I have already stated, reproached the Moscow action group for being slow and not sufficiently active.

"In giving the reasons for the necessity of committing a terroristic act against *Kirov, Zinoviev* said that *Kirov* must be physically destroyed as *Stalin's* closest assistant. He also added: 'It is not enough to fell the oak; all the young oaks growing around it must be felled too.' Another argument *Zinoviev* used in support of the necessity of murdering *Kirov* was that *Kirov* was the leader of the Leningrad organization and was personally responsible for the rout of the opposition in Leningrad.

"As I have already stated, the Leningrad fighting organization was under the direct leadership of *Bakayev*. Organizational connection with this organization was also maintained by *Faivilovich*." (Vol. XXVII, p. 70.)

After persistent denials of his participation in the organization of the assassination of Comrade *Kirov*, the accused *Bakayev*, under the weight of evidence brought against him, testified:

"I admit that *Zinoviev* personally instructed me to organize the assassination of *Stalin* in Moscow, and *Karev* to organize the assassination of *Kirov* in Leningrad. For this purpose I instructed *Karev* to establish contact in Leningrad with *Vladimir Levin* and *Anishev*, members of the organization, while *Zinoviev* instructed me to put *Karev* in touch also with *Rumyantsev* in Leningrad." (Vol. I, p. 89.)

Evidence on the role played by *Bakayev* as one of the principal organizers of the assassination of Comrade *Kirov* was also given by *N. A. Karev*, who is under arrest in connection with another case. At the examination held on July 5, 1936, *N. A. Karev* stated:

"*Zinoviev* said that *Bakayev* had been charged with the preparation of terroristic acts against *Stalin* and *Kirov* and that for this purpose he was to utilize his connections with the Zinovievite groups in Leningrad and Moscow."

To this *Karev* added:

"In conversation with *Bakayev*, I learned that the latter intended to utilize the Zinovievite groups of *Rumyantsev* and *Kotolynov* in Leningrad with which he, *Bakayev*, had contact, for the organization of a terroristic act against *Kirov*."

(Vol. III, p. 11.)

This was also fully confirmed during the investigation by the accused *Evdokimov*, who stated the following:

"I learned from *Bakayev* that in the autumn of 1934, he, *Bakayev*, together with one Trotskyite terrorist, whose name

33

I do not know, went to Leningrad to establish contact with the Leningrad terrorist centre and to organize the assassination of *Kirov*.

"While in Leningrad, *Bakayev* and the above-mentioned Trotskyite terrorist met *Nikolayev* and arranged with him that he would assassinate *Kirov*."

(Vol. XXXVI, pp. 7, 8.)

And further:

"*Bakayev* stated that the terrorists had expressed confidence in the success of the terroristic act; they considered themselves to be safe. The reason for this was that all of them, including such active Zinovievites as *Rumyantsev, Levin, Myasnikov, Mandelstamm* and others, enjoyed the confidence of a number of leading Party workers and officials of Soviet organizations in Leningrad. This ensured them every possibility of pursuing their preparations for a terroristic act against *Kirov* without the least fear of being discovered."

(Vol. XXXVI, p. 9.)

The investigation has established that after the united Zinovievite-Trotskyite centre had adopted the decision to assassinate Comrade *S. M. Kirov, Kamenev* made a special journey to Leningrad in June 1934 for checking up on the progress of the work of organizing the terroristic act against Comrade *Kirov*.

Zinoviev also pressed forward in every way the assassination of Comrade *Kirov* and, as testified by *N. M. Matorin*, formerly *Zinoviev's* private secretary, who is now under arrest in connection with another case, *Zinoviev* reproached the members of the terrorist group for being slow and irresolute.

Matorin testified:

"*Zinoviev* told me that the preparations for the terroristic act must be pressed forward to the utmost and that *Kirov* must be killed by the winter. *Zinoviev* reproached me for not displaying sufficient determination and energy. He said that with regard to terroristic methods of struggle prejudices must be dropped." (Vol. XIV, pp. 63, 64.)

III. Organization by the United Trotskyite-Zinovievite Centre of Terroristic Acts Against Comrades Voroshilov, Zhdanov, Kaganovich, Kossior, Orjonikidze and Postyshev

The materials of the investigation have established that the united Trotskyite-Zinovievite terrorist centre, after it had killed Comrade *Kirov*, did not confine itself to organizing the assassination of Comrade *Stalin* alone. The terrorist Trotskyite-Zinovievite centre simultaneously carried on work to organize assassinations of other leaders of the Party, namely, Comrades *Voroshilov, Zhdanov, Kaganovich, Kossior, Orjonikidze* and *Postyshev.*

The accused *Reingold* testified that *Zinoviev*, while speaking of the necessity of assassinating Comrade *Kirov* as Comrade *Stalin's* closest assistant, added:

> "It is not enough to fell the oak; all the young oaks growing around it must be felled too."   (Vol. XXVII, p. 70.)

According to *Reingold's* testimony:

> "*Zinoviev's* main instructions amounted to the following: the blow must be directed against *Stalin, Kaganovich* and *Kirov.*"   (Vol. XXVII, p. 63.)

The accused *Reingold* confirmed that:

> "The expectations of the united centre were based on a plan to cause complete confusion in the Party and in the country by a stunning simultaneous blow in Moscow and Leningrad."   (Vol. XXVII, p. 163.)

Various terrorist groups operating under the general leadership of the united centre attempted to carry out the assassinations of *Voroshilov, Kaganovich, Zhdanov, Kossior, Orjonikidze* and *Postyshev.*

Thus, the organization of the terroristic act against Comrade *Voroshilov* was the work of *Dreitzer's* group, which received instructions to murder *Voroshilov* directly from *Trotsky,* and of the group of the Trotskyite *M. Lurye,* which was sent over from Germany for the same purpose.

In regard to the preparations for the assassination of Comrade *Voroshilov,* the accused *Mrachkovsky,* one of the members of the united centre testified:

"In the middle of 1934, *E. Dreitzer* reported to me that simultaneously he was organizing the assassination of *Voro- ·shilov,* for which purpose Dimitri *Schmidt,* who was a commander in the army and under no suspicion in the Party, was to be prepared. It was presumed that he would kill *Voroshilov* either while reporting to him on service matters, or during the next manoeuvres at which *Voroshilov* would be present." (Vol. XVIII, p. 49.)

The accused *Dreitzer,* examined at the office of the State Attorney of the Soviet Union on July 31, testified on this point:

"For the purpose of committing the terroristic act I recruited *Esterman* and *Gayevsky,* and in 1935 *Schmidt* and *Kuzmichev.* The latter two undertook to kill *Voroshilov.*" (Vol. X, p. 195.)

The testimony of *Mrachkovsky* and *Dreitzer* was also confirmed by the accused *Reingold,* who testified as follows:

"I learned from *Mrachkovsky* and *Dreitzer* that in the summer of 1933 a Trotskyite group of military men was organized under the leadership of *Dreitzer.* The group consisted of *Schmidt,* commander of a brigade of the Red Army, *Kuzmichev,* chief of staff of a military unit, and a number of other persons whose names I do not know. I learned from *Dreitzer* that *Schmidt* and *Kuzmichev* were to carry out personally the terroristic act against *Voroshilov* and that they had agreed to do so. It was planned that for this purpose they would either take advantage of an official reception by *Voroshilov,* or of *Voroshilov's* visit to one of their military units." (Vol. XXVII, pp. 165, 166.)

The investigation has also established that in the same period, a number of terrorist groups (those of *Dreitzer, M. Lurye* and others) were organizing attempts on the lives of Comrades *Zhdanov, Kaganovich, Orjonikidze, Kossior* and *Postyshev.*

36

Definition of the Charge

Analyzing the above, the investigating authorities consider it established:

1) That in the period of 1932-1936 a united Trotskyite-Zinovievite centre was organized in the city of Moscow with the object of committing a number of terroristic acts against the leaders of the C.P.S.U. and the Soviet Government for the purpose of seizing power.

2) That of those accused in the present case, *G. E. Zinoviev, L. B. Kamenev, G. E. Evdokimov* and *I. P. Bakayev* entered the united Trotskyite-Zinovievite centre from the Zinovievites and *I. N. Smirnov, V. A. Ter-Vaganyan* and *S. V. Mrachkovsky* from the Trotskyites.

3) That during this period, the united Trotskyite-Zinovievite centre organized a number of terrorist groups and prepared a number of practical measures to assassinate Comrades *Stalin, Voroshilov, Zhdanov, Kaganovich, Kirov, Kossior, Orjonikidze* and *Postyshev.*

4) That one of these terrorist groups, operating on the direct instructions of *Zinoviev* and *L. Trotsky* and of the united Trotskyite-Zinovievite centre, and under the immediate direction of the accused *Bakayev,* carried out the foul murder of Comrade *S. M. Kirov* on December 1, 1934.

The accused in this case: *G. E. Zinoviev, L. B. Kamenev, G. E. Evdokimov, I. P. Bakayev, V. A. Ter-Vaganyan, S. V. Mrachkovsky, E. A. Dreitzer, V. P. Olberg, Fritz David (I. I. Kruglyansky), E. S. Holtzman, R. V. Pickel, I. I. Reingold, K. B. Berman-Yurin, M. Lurye* and *N. Lurye* have fully admitted their guilt of the charges preferred against them.

The accused *I. N. Smïrnov,* acknowledging his participation in the united centre of the Trotskyite-Zinovievite *bloc,* his personal connection with *L. Trotsky* and his meetings with *L. Sedov* while abroad in 1931, and also the fact that he maintained connection with *Trotsky* right up to the time of his arrest in 1933, admitted that in 1931 instructions were conveyed to him by *Sedov,* and confirmed in 1932 by *Trotsky* to organize terror against the leaders of the C.P.S.U. and the Soviet State and that these instructions

37

served as the basis of the organization of the Trotskyite-Zinovievite *bloc.*

At the same time, the accused *I. N. Smirnov* categorically denies that he took part in the terroristic activities of the united Trotskyite-Zinovievite centre. However, the accused *I. N. Smirnov* is proved to have participated in the terroristic activities of the united centre by the evidence of the accused *S. V. Mrachkovsky* (Vol. XXIX, pages 76-84), *E. A. Dreitzer* (Vol. XXXI, page 63), *A. N. Safonova* (Vol. XXXI, page 295), *I. I. Reingold* (Vol. XXXI pages 138, 284), *G. E. Zinoviev* (Vol. XII, page 35), *L. B. Kamenev* (Vol. XV, page 28), *G. E. Evdokimov* (Vol. XXXVI, pages 9, 10), *R. V. Pickel* (Vol. XXXI, page 78).

On the basis of the above:

1. *Zinoviev,* Grigori Evseyevich, born in 1883, employee, convicted in 1935 in the Zinovievite "Moscow centre" case;

2. *Kamenev,* Lev Borisovich, born in 1883, employee, convicted in 1935 in the same "Moscow centre" case;

3. *Evdokimov,* Grigori Eremeyevich, born in 1884, employee, convicted in 1935 in the same "Moscow centre" case;

4. *Bakayev,* Ivan Petrovich, born in 1887, employee, convicted in 1935 in the same "Moscow centre" case;

5. *Mrachkovsky,* Sergei Vitalevich, born in 1888, employee;

6. *Ter-Vaganyan,* Vagarshak Arutyunovich, born in 1893, employee;

7. *Smirnov,* Ivan Nikitich, born in 1880, employee
—are accused of having, the first six in the period of 1932 to 1936, and *I. N. Smirnov* since 1931

a) organized a number of terrorist groups which were making preparations to assassinate Comrades *Stalin, Voroshilov, Zhdanov, Kaganovich. Kirov, Kossior, Orjonikidze* and *Postyshev;*

b) organized and carried out on Dec. 1, 1934, the foul murder of Comrade *S. M. Kirov,* through the Leningrad underground terrorist group of *Nikolayev-Kotolynov* and others;

i.e., of crimes covered by Articles 58^8 and 58^{11} of the Criminal Code of the R.S.F.S.R.

8. *Dreitzer,* Ephim Alexandrovich, born in 1894, employee;

9. *Reingold,* Isak Isayevich, born in 1897, employee;

10. *Pickel,* Richard Vitoldovich, born in 1896, employee;

11. *Holtzman,* Edouard Solomonovich, born in 1882, employee,

12. *David,* Fritz, alias *Kruglyansky,* Ilya-David Israilevich, born in 1897, employee;

13. *Olberg,* Valentine Pavlovich, born in 1907, employee;

14. *Berman-Yurin,* Konon Borisovich (alias Alexander *Fomich*), born in 1901, employee;

15. *Lurye,*Moissei Ilyich (alias Alexander *Emel*),born in1897, employee;

16. *Lurye,* Nathan Lazarevich, born in 1901, employee

—are accused of that, being members of the underground terrorist Trotskyite-Zinovievite organization, they took part in the preparations to assassinate Comrades *Stalin, Voroshilov, Zhdanov, Kaganovich, Kossior, Orjonikidze* and *Postyshev;*

i.e., crimes covered by Articles 19 and 58^8, 58^{11} of the Criminal Code of the R.S.F.S.R.

L. Trotsky and his son *L. L. Sedov,* both of whom are abroad, having been exposed by the materials in the present case as having directly prepared and personally guided the work of organizing in the U.S.S.R. terroristic acts against the leaders of the C.P.S.U. and of the Soviet State, in the event of their being discovered on the territory of the U.S.S.R., are subject to immediate arrest and trial by the Military Collegium of the Supreme Court of the U.S.S.R.

The cases of *Gertik, Grinberg, Y. Gaven, Karev, Kuzmichev, Konstant, Matorin,* Paul *Olberg, Radin, Safonova, Faivilovich, D. Schmidt,* and *Esterman,* in view of the fact that investigation is still proceeding, have been set aside for separate trial.

In view of the above and in accordance with the decision of the Central Executive Committee of the U.S.S.R. of Aug. 11, 1936, all the above-mentioned persons are subject to trial by the Military Collegium of the Supreme Court of the U.S.S.R. in open court session.

The present indictment was drawn up in the city of Moscow on Aug. 14, 1936.

A. VYSHINSKY
State Attorney of the U.S.S.R.

After the reading of the indictment, the President of the Court questions in turn all the accused whether they plead guilty as charged. The accused Zinoviev, Kamenev, Evdokimov, Bakayev, Ter-Vaganyan, Mrachkovsky, Dreitzer, Reingold, Pickel, Olberg, Berman-Yurin, Fritz David (Kruglyansky), M. Lurye and N. Lurye plead guilty on all charges. The accused I. N. Smirnov, admitting that he belonged to the united centre of the Trotskyite-Zinovievite *bloc*, that he had been in personal communication with Trotsky and had received Trotsky's instructions to organize terror against the leaders of the C.P.S.U. and the Soviet State, and admitting his political responsibility for the activities of the united centre, denies only his personal participation in the preparation and execution of terroristic acts.

The accused Holtzman admits having belonged to the Trotskyite-Zinovievite terrorist organization, having been in personal contact with the Trotskyite centre abroad, and having brought Trotsky's personal instructions to organize terroristic acts in the U.S.S.R. He denies only his own personal participation in the preparation of terroristic acts.

After a recess of 15 minutes, the court at 1:45 p.m. proceeds to examine the accused.

EXAMINATION OF THE ACCUSED MRACHKOVSKY

The accused Mrachkovsky was the man most in the confidence of Trotsky and personally closest to him. In the past he had occupied an important position in the army. From 1923 onwards he had carried on, in conjunction with Trotsky, Trotskyite anti-Soviet work. He had been a member of the leading centre of the underground Trotskyite terrorist organization, had worked under the personal direction of Trotsky, from whom he was receiving instructions through I. N. Smirnov as well as directly to organize terroristic acts against the leaders of the Party and the Government. Being one of the leaders of the counter-revolutionary Trotskyite underground organization, he, in 1932, had joined the united Trotskyite-Zinovievite terrorist centre together with I. N. Smirnov and V. A. Ter-Vaganyan.

Mrachkovsky relates in detail the history of the formation of the Trotskyite-Zinovievite terrorist centre. He says that on returning from exile in 1929 he only on paper admitted the correctness of the general line of the Party; actually, however, together with other former members of the opposition, he returned from exile with the perfidious intention of continuing the struggle against the Party. Asked by Comrade Vyshinsky to say definitely to whom he was referring, Mrachkovsky said that he, Mrachkovsky, and also I. N. Smirnov and Ter-Vaganyan, had jointly taken the firm decision to organize a further struggle against the Party. Mrachkovsky at the same time admits that this counter-revolutionary group had no political platform, that "the platform drawn up in the preceding period of 1925-27 was upset by the fact of the correctness of the general line of the Party."

Mrachkovsky goes on to say that already in 1931 this Trotskyite group openly discussed the question of terrorism. I. N. Smirnov, who had visited Berlin, brought back instructions from Trotsky, which he received through Trotsky's son, L. Sedov, to the following effect: "Until we put Stalin out of the way, we shall not be able to come back to power."

Vyshinsky: What do you mean by the expression: "Until we put Stalin out of the way"?

Mrachkovsky: Until we kill Stalin. At that very meeting, in the presence of Smirnov, myself, Ter-Vaganyan and Safonova, I was given the task of organizing a terrorist group, that is to say, to select reliable people. The same task was assigned to Dreitzer together with me. That period, 1931 and 1932, was spent in inducing and preparing people to commit terroristic acts. For this purpose I recruited Yatsek and Yudin. Dreitzer recruited another group of people including Schmidt, Kuzmichev and some others whom I don't remember. As I have already said, this period was spent in preparing people for organizing terroristic acts against Stalin, Voroshilov and Kaganovich.

Mrachkovsky goes on to state that in the second half of 1932 the question was raised of the necessity of uniting the Trotskyite terrorist group with the Zinovievites. The question of this unification was raised by I. N. Smirnov who, in doing so, argued that the Trotskyite forces by themselves were too weak and that therefore it was necessary to unite all counter-revolutionary groups. It was at that time that Smirnov sent a letter to Trotsky through Holtz-

41

man in which he informed Trotsky of the state of the Trotskyite organization and put before him the question of uniting with the Zinovievites. In the autumn of 1932 a letter was received from Trotsky in which he approved the decision to unite with the Zinovievites. It was also at that time that Trotsky conveyed to them through his emissary, Gaven, that union must take place on the basis of terrorism, and Trotsky once again emphasized the necessity of killing Stalin, Voroshilov and Kirov.

Vyshinsky: Another question to Smirnov. Do you corroborate the testimony of Mrachkovsky that in 1932 you received a reply from Trotsky through Gaven?

Smirnov: I received a reply from Trotsky through Gaven.

Vyshinsky: And in addition, did you receive verbal information on the conversation with Trotsky?

Smirnov: Yes, also verbal conversation.

Vyshinsky: You, Smirnov, confirm before the Supreme Court that in 1932 you received from Gaven the direction from Trotsky to commit acts of terrorism?

Smirnov: Yes.

Vyshinsky: Against whom?

Smirnov: Against the leaders.

Vyshinsky: Against which?

Smirnov: Stalin and others.

Continuing his testimony, Mrachkovsky observed that after receiving the instructions from Trotsky approving the formation of a *bloc* with the Zinovievites, Smirnov instructed Ter-Vaganyan to bring about the formation of this *bloc*. The terrorist *bloc* of the Trotskyites and the Zinovievites was formed at the end of 1932. Mrachkovsky related that before his departure from Moscow in 1932, Smirnov had asked him to see Reingold, who was leading the Moscow terrorist group, and to come to an agreement with him about uniting all forces.

Vyshinsky: On what basis?

Mrachkovsky: On the basis of organizing the assassination of Stalin.

Vyshinsky: Smirnov said: Go to Reingold and come to an agreement with him about ...

Mrachkovsky: ... Uniting our terrorist forces for the purpose of assassinating Stalin, Voroshilov and Kaganovich.

Mrachkovsky goes on to say that on his departure from Moscow he instructed Reingold to get in touch with Dreitzer who was to direct the terroristic activities of the Moscow centre. On arriving in Moscow again in the summer of 1934 he met Dreitzer who informed him about the work of the terrorist centre. Questioned by Comrade Vyshinsky, Dreitzer confirms this statement by Mrachkovsky. Mrachkovsky goes on to say that Dreitzer informed him about the organization of the Moscow terrorist centre of the Trotskyite-Zinovievite *bloc,* consisting of himself, *i.e.,* Dreitzer, and also Reingold and Pickel. Questioned by Comrade Vyshinsky, Reingold and Pickel confirm the statement that they were members of the Moscow terrorist centre.

In the summer of 1934 Mrachkovsky met Kamenev. "Kamenev," testifies Mrachkovsky, "confirmed to me the fact that a Moscow terrorist centre had been organized. Kamenev expressed dissatisfaction with the slowness with which the work of preparing terroristic acts was proceeding. During this conversation he said that Bakayev was organizing in Leningrad, apparently very successfully, although slowly, a terroristic act against Kirov."

Continuing his testimony, Mrachkovsky states that in December 1934, while in Kazakhstan, he received from Dreitzer a letter of Trotsky's, written in invisible ink, which had approximately the following contents—Dear friend, the task that confronts us today is to accelerate the assassination of Stalin and Voroshilov. In the event of war, it is necessary to adopt a defeatist position and take advantage of the confusion. Nuclei must be organized in the Red Army. The letter was signed "Starik" (old man).

Mrachkovsky emphasizes the fact that he knew Trotsky's handwriting very well and that he had not the slightest doubt that the letter had actually been written by Trotsky. Emphasizing that he stood particularly close to Trotsky, Mrachkovsky states that during the last few years of his work with Trotsky, in 1923-27, no one could get to see Trotsky without him, Mrachkovsky, and also that all Trotsky's correspondence passed through his hands.

Comrade Vyshinsky asks Mrachkovsky what role I. N. Smirnov played in the terrorist Trotskyite-Zinovievite centre. Mrachkovsky emphasizes that he, Mrachkovsky, did everything with the knowledge of Smirnov and that Smirnov knew the people whom he, Mrachkovsky, was preparing to commit terroristic acts.

Questioned by Comrade Vyshinsky whether he confirms Mrachkovsky's testimony, Smirnov asserts that Mrachkovsky's statements do not conform with the facts.

Vyshinsky: You were a member of the Trotskyite-Zinovievite centre. That you admit. Here Mrachkovsky is not sinning against the truth. That is the first point. Secondly, the centre was organized on the basis of terrorism against the leaders of the Party and the government. Is that right?

Smirnov: That is right.

Vyshinsky: Did you receive from Trotsky instructions on terrorism as a means of struggle?

Smirnov: Yes.

Mrachkovsky then goes on to tell the Court about the activities of the Trotskyite-Zinovievite terrorist centre. The members of this centre were Zinoviev, Kamenev, Lominadze, Mrachkovsky, Ter-Vaganyan and others.

Comrade Vyshinsky then asks Zinoviev:

Vyshinsky: When was the united centre organized?

Zinoviev: In the summer of 1932.

Vyshinsky: During what period of time did it function?

Zinoviev: Actually up to 1936.

Vyshinsky: What were its activities?

Zinoviev: Its main activities consisted in making preparations for terroristic acts.

Vyshinsky: Against whom?

Zinoviev: Against the leaders.

Vyshinsky: That is, against Comrades Stalin, Voroshilov, and Kaganovich? Was it your centre that organized the assassination of Comrade Kirov? Was the assassination of Sergei Mironovich Kirov organized by your centre, or by some other organization?

Zinoviev: Yes, by our centre.

Vyshinsky: In that centre there were you, Kamenev, Smirnov, Mrachkovsky and Ter-Vaganyan?

Zinoviev: Yes.

Vyshinsky: So you all organized the assassination of Kirov?

44

Zinoviev: Yes.

Vyshinsky: So you all assassinated Comrade Kirov?

Zinoviev: Yes.

Vyshinsky: Sit down.

In connection with Mrachkovsky's testimony, the accused Ter-Vaganyan is examined. He admits that negotiations for the formation of a united Trotskyite-Zinovievite terrorist *bloc* were started as far back as June 1932 and that in the first stages of the negotiations he, Ter-Vaganyan, had served as intermediary between Lominadze and Kamenev, and between Smirnov and Zinoviev.

I. N. Smirnov denies Mrachkovsky's testimony to the effect that he, Smirnov, had conveyed Trotsky's instructions about terrorism to the Moscow Trotskyite centre.

Vyshinsky: I ask leave to read Vol. XXIX, p. 115, of the record of the examination of Smirnov on August 13 by Scheinin, Examining Magistrate for cases of special importance, according to which Smirnov said that in 1931 Sedov gave terroristic directions. Here is Smirnov's testimony: "On my return to Moscow I reported this to Safonova and Mrachkovsky."

Vyshinsky: Well, now, does this correspond to what you said five minutes ago?

Smirnov: (Remains silent.)

Vyshinsky: I ask that permission be given to Smirnov himself to read this passage from the evidence. As Smirnov persists in his denials, tries to evade responsibility, I ask that he read this passage from the evidence in front of everybody present here.

Smirnov (reading his testimony): "In 1931 Sedov gave terroristic directions which, on my return to Moscow, I reported to Safonova and Mrachkovsky."

Vyshinsky (to Mrachkovsky): Mrachkovsky, did you learn about Sedov's line on terrorism from Smirnov?

Mrachkovsky: Yes.

Vyshinsky: After Smirnov's return from Berlin did you meet him?

Mrachkovsky: Yes.

Vyshinsky: Did you speak to him?

Mrachkovsky: Yes.

45

Vyshinsky: Together with Safonova?

Mrachkovsky: Yes.

Vyshinsky: And you knew about these directions of Sedov's?

Mrachkovsky: Yes, I so affirm.

Vyshinsky: Smirnov, did you hear that?

Smirnov: (Remains silent.)

In reply to the questions of Comrade Ulrich, President of the Court, Smirnov admits that he also communicated Trotsky's instructions to Ter-Vaganyan. In reply to Comrade Vyshinsky, the accused Kamenev once again states that "the instructions Smirnov had personally received from Trotsky—the directions on terrorism—had been passed on as given by Smirnov and that they were of decisive importance to the organization."

At the end of Mrachkovsky's examination Vyshinsky asks Bakayev in what part of 1934 he went to Leningrad.

Bakayev: In the autumn.

Vyshinsky: For what purpose?

Bakayev: To ascertain the preparedness of the organization to assassinate Kirov.

Vyshinsky (to Kamenev): Did you give the instructions to make preparations for the assassination of Kirov?

Kamenev: Yes, in the autumn.

Vyshinsky: In the autumn you and Evdokimov instructed Bakayev to go to Leningrad to check up on the progress which was being made by the Leningrad Trotskyite-Zinovievite group in its preparations to assassinate Kirov? Is that right; do you confirm that?

Kamenev: Yes, that is true. I confirm that.

EXAMINATION OF THE ACCUSED EVDOKIMOV

Questioned by Comrade Ulrich, President of the Court, whether he confirms the testimony he gave at the preliminary examination, Evdokimov replies in the affirmative. After that Evdokimov answers a number of questions put to him by Comrade Vyshinsky.

Vyshinsky: You were a member of the centre?

Evdokimov: Yes, I was.

46

Vyshinsky: Did you know that the centre was preparing assassinations of the leaders of the C.P.S.U. and the Soviet Government?

Evdokimov: Yes.

Vyshinsky: Did you personally approve of the preparation of these assassinations?

Evdokimov: I agreed to them.

Vyshinsky: You took part in and considered it necessary to proceed by the path of assassination?

Evdokimov: Yes.

Vyshinsky: Do you admit that the assassination of Comrade Kirov was prepared with your assistance?

Evdokimov: Yes, I admit that.

Vyshinsky: At the trial in Leningrad, on January 15-16, 1935, when facing the court as you do now, you emphatically asserted that you had nothing to do with that murder. At that time you told untruths?

Evdokimov: Yes, I deceived the Court.

Vyshinsky: You thought you deceived the Court. As a matter of fact the deception did not work. Now it is exposed.

Evdokimov: Yes.

After that Evdokimov relates to the Court in detail that the assassination of S. M. Kirov was committed on the direct instructions of the terrorist centre of the Trotzkyite-Zinovievite organization. The instructions about terrorism came from Trotsky. "Smirnov and I," says Evdokimov, "discussed this question several times. In the summer of 1932, a conference was held in the railway car of Mrachkovsky who had just arrived in Moscow. I, Mrachkovsky, Smirnov and Ter-Vaganyan were present at this conference. We talked of terrorism, Smirnov, particularly, was in favour of terrorism."

Smirnov makes the attempt to deny this testimony of Evdokimov. However, the replies of Mrachkovsky and Evdokimov to questions put to them by Comrade Vyshinsky establish that the conversation about terrorism did take place and that Smirnov fully and completely supported the line of terroristic acts.

Soon after this conversation in Mrachkovsky's car, says Evdokimov, continuing his testimony, a conference took place in the summer villa at Ilyinskoye, where Kamenev and Zinoviev lived at that time. At this conference, at which Karev, Zinoviev, Kamenev, Evdokimov and Bakayev were present, it was decided to form a Moscow centre and a Leningrad centre for the purpose of combining the terrorist groups. And this decision was subsequently put into effect. At this same conference at Ilyinskoye in 1932, there was outright talk about the necessity of terrorism, in the first place against Stalin and Kirov. The organization of these terroristic acts was, on Zinoviev's proposal, entrusted to Bakayev.

Vyshinsky: Accused Bakayev, do you confirm this?

Bakayev: During that conference Zinoviev said that the Trotskyites, on Trotsky's proposal, had set to work to organize the assassination of Stalin and that we should take the initiative in this matter into our own hands.

Vyshinsky: Zinoviev said that?

Bakayev: Yes.

Vyshinsky. Zinoviev said that you should take the initiative?

Bakayev: At that conference I was instructed to organize a terroristic act against Stalin.

Vyshinsky: And you undertook to do that, did you?

Bakayev: Yes.

Continuing, Evdokimov states with reference to the facts concerning the preparations for the assassination of S. M. Kirov, that in the summer of 1934 a conference was held in Kamenev's apartment in Moscow at which Kamenev, Zinoviev, Evdokimov, Sokolnikov, Ter-Vaganyan, Reingold and Bakayev were present. At this conference it was decided to expedite the assassination of S. M. Kirov.

Vyshinsky: So it was put as straight as that: "To expedite the assassination of S. M. Kirov"?

Evdokimov: Yes, it was put like that.

Continuing, Evdokimov says that for this purpose Bakayev, in the autumn of 1934, went to Leningrad to check up on the progress of preparations for the terroristic act against Sergei Mironovich Kirov by the Leningrad terrorists. These terrorist groups began to shadow Sergei Mironovich Kirov and waited for an opportune moment to commit their terroristic act.

Vyshinsky: Was the murder of Sergei Mironovich Kirov prepared by the centre?

Evdokimov: Yes.

Vyshinsky: You personally took part in these preparations?

Evdokimov: Yes.

Vyshinsky: Did Zinoviev and Kamenev participate with you in the preparations?

Evdokimov: Yes.

Vyshinsky: On the instructions of the centre, Bakayev went to Leningrad to check up on the progress made in the preparations, did he not?

Evdokimov: Yes.

As a result of further questioning Comrade Vyshinsky establishes that while on his visit to Leningrad, Bakayev met the future murderer of S. M. Kirov, Nikolayev, with whom he discussed the preparations for the assassination.

Vyshinsky (to Bakayev): Did you meet Nikolayev in Leningrad?

Bakayev: Yes.

Vyshinsky: Did you confer about an understanding regarding the assassination of S. M. Kirov?

Bakayev: There was no need for me to come to an understanding with him about it because the instructions for the assassination had been given by Zinoviev and Kamenev.

Vyshinsky: But Nikolayev told you that he had decided to assassinate S. M. Kirov, didn't he?

Bakayev: He did, and so did other terrorists—Levin, Mandelstamm, Kotolynov, Rumyantsev.

Vyshinsky: You discussed the assassination of Kirov?

Bakayev: Yes.

Vyshinsky: He expressed his determination. And what was your attitude towards it?

Bakayev: I was for it.

In reply to further questions put by Comrade Vyshinsky to Bakayev it is ascertained that after his visit to Leningrad, Bakayev reported to Evdokimov and Kamenev on the progress

49

of the preparations for the assassination of S. M. Kirov. Asked by Comrade Vyshinsky whether Bakayev had actually reported to him, Kamenev answered in the affirmative.

Vyshinsky (to Kamenev): What did he report to you?

Kamenev: He said that the organization was prepared to strike a blow and that the blow would be struck.

Vyshinsky: And what was your attitude towards this?

Kamenev: The blow was planned and prepared on the order of the centre of which I was a member, and I regarded it as the fulfilment of the task we had set ourselves.

*   *   *

This concludes the morning session.

AUGUST 19 (EVENING SESSION)

EXAMINATION OF THE ACCUSED DREITZER

The first to be examined at the evening session of August 19 is the accused Dreitzer. Dreitzer was one of the most prominent Trotskyites. He had been chief of Trotsky's bodyguard. Together with Trotsky, he had organized the counter-revolutionary demonstration on November 7, 1927. When Trotsky was in exile in Alma-Ata, Dreitzer organized the communications between Trotsky and the Moscow Trotskyite centre.

The accused Dreitzer states that the Trotskyite-Zinovievite underground organization was a strictly centralized and disciplined counter-revolutionary organization. Dreitzer categorically and emphatically denies that there could be any possibility of half-heartedness in the attitude of any one of the members of the Trotskyite-Zinovievite counter-revolutionary *bloc* towards terroristic activity.

"There could be no acting on one's own, no orchestra without a conductor among us," stated Dreitzer. "I am surprised at the assertions of Smirnov, who, according to his words, both knew and did not know, spoke and did not speak, acted and did not act. This is not true!"

Relating his terroristic activities in detail Dreitzer says that the Trotskyite section of the counter-revolutionary *bloc* had received instructions to resort to terrorism against the leaders of the Party and the government from abroad, from L. D. Trotsky, and here from I. N. Smirnov, Trotsky's deputy in the U.S.S.R.

In the autumn of 1931, Dreitzer took advantage of an official business trip to Berlin to establish contact with Trotsky at the instructions from I. N. Smirnov.

Smirnov's definite instructions were to ascertain Trotsky's attitude on the question of a *bloc* between the Trotskyites and the Zinovievites. In Berlin he twice met Sedov (Trotsky's son), in a café in Leipziger Strasse. Sedov then told him that Trotsky's instruction would be sent on later.

In October 1934 Dreitzer's sister brought him from Warsaw a German cinema magazine which an agent of Sedov's had given her for Dreitzer. In the magazine Dreitzer had no difficulty in discovering—as this form of communication had been agreed upon with Sedov in Berlin—a message written in invisible ink in Trotsky's own handwriting containing instructions to prepare and to carry out immediately terroristic acts against Stalin and Voroshilov. Dreitzer at once passed the letter on to Mrachkovsky who, after reading it, burnt it for reasons of secrecy.

As far back as September-October 1931 I. N. Smirnov had spoken to Dreitzer in the U.S.S.R. about the necessity to follow the line of terroristic methods of struggle. In the autumn of 1932, Dreitzer received from I. N. Smirnov, in the latter's apartment, direct instructions to organize terroristic acts against Stalin and Voroshilov. Smirnov, referring to the line taken by Trotsky, there and then instructed Dreitzer to establish contact with Mrachkovsky for the purpose of making practical preparations for and carrying out terroristic acts. "My next meeting with Ivan Nikitich Smirnov," said Dreitzer, "took place in 1932. This was in the autumn. At that meeting he informed me that the question of a *bloc* had been settled, that the *bloc* had already been formed, and had been formed on the basis of Trotsky's terroristic line."

In the spring of 1933 Mrachkovsky repeated to Dreitzer the instructions of the Trotskyite-Zinovievite centre to expedite the acts of terror against the leaders of the C.P.S.U. and the Soviet Government. Moreover, on leaving Moscow, Mrachkovsky put at Dreitzer's disposal a number of terrorists he had trained. In addition to Smirnov and Mrachkovsky, Dreitzer was very closely connected with Reingold and Pickel, together with whom he belonged to the Moscow terrorist centre of the Trotskyite-Zinovievite *bloc.*

Carrying out the instructions of L. D. Trotsky and the Trotskyite-Zinovievite terrorist centre, conveyed to him by Smirnov and Mrachkovsky, Dreitzer organized two terrorist groups: Gayevsky's

52

group, which was instructed to commit a terroristic act against Comrade Stalin, and Esterman's group, which was instructed to kill Comrade Voroshilov.

In connection with Dreitzer's evidence the State Prosecutor questions Mrachkovsky and I. N. Smirnov.

Mrachkovsky fully confirms Dreitzer's testimony.

Smirnov asserts that he actually did receive in his apartment Dreitzer as an active Trotskyite; however, he allegedly discussed with him, not terrorism but "the general situation in the country."

Mrachkovsky and Dreitzer in reply to this declare: "Smirnov is lying!"

Upon the conclusion of Dreitzer's examination Comrade Vyshinsky puts several questions to the accused Zinoviev.

Vyshinsky: Accused Zinoviev, in the summer of 1932 had you already come to an understanding about the necessity of organizing terroristic acts, or was there only talk about these terroristic acts?

Zinoviev: As far as I can picture it, the situation was as follows: With the Trotskyites this was already a mature decision, based on the absolutely precise instructions of Trotsky given a fairly long time before that, and they had taken a number of practical steps.

Vyshinsky: What was the attitude of the Trotskyite part of your *bloc* on the question of terrorism?

Zinoviev: In our negotiations on the formation of a united centre this question played a decisive part. By that time the so-called Zinovievite part of the *bloc* was fully ripe for such decisions.

Vyshinsky: Did Smirnov display any activity in relation to this, or not?

Zinoviev: Smirnov, in my opinion, displayed more activity than any one else, and we regarded him as the undisputed head of the Trotskyite part of the *bloc,* as the man best informed about Trotsky's views, and fully sharing these views.

Vyshinsky: Did you personally hear a number of proposals from Smirnov?

Zinoviev: I personally conducted negotiations with him two or three times.

Vyshinsky: Did Smirnov display persistence during these negotiations, did he press for terroristic acts?

Zinoviev: As I have already said, he heatedly and with much persuasion insisted on the commission of terroristic acts, although there was no need to persuade us. We were already convinced.

Vyshinsky: I ask the court to note that the testimony of Zinoviev, Reingold and Dreitzer establishes that after 1932 practical preparations were made for terroristic acts, and that Dreitzer carried these on on the direct instructions of Smirnov; and that Smirnov persistently urged Zinoviev to pass on to terroristic activities. I ask you to take note of this as a conclusion to be drawn from the investigation which we have carried on so far.

EXAMINATION OF THE ACCUSED REINGOLD

I. I. Reingold confirms that he was one of the most active members of the Zinovievite underground counter-revolutionary organization, was all the time in direct contact with G. E. Zinoviev and L. B. Kamenev, took part in all the secret conferences of the Zinovievites and at one time was invited by Zinoviev and Kamenev to take part in drawing up the platform of the counter-revolutionary organization they were heading, was a member of the Moscow Trotskyite-Zinovievite centre, organizer of terroristic groups and personally directed one of the groups which was preparing to assassinate Comrade Stalin.

Reingold says: "I was connected organizationally and personally with a number of members of the Trotskyite-Zinovievite centre: Zinoviev, Kamenev, Sokolnikov and others. With some of these I was connected long before 1926. In particular I have been acquainted with Kamenev since 1923 and with Sokolnikov since 1919. As for the Trotskyite part of this centre, Dreitzer was my personal friend; I was in very close touch with Mrachkovsky at my official job, as Mrachkovsky worked under me at the head offices of the Central Cotton Committee. I also knew I. N. Smirnov very well. I was in close contact also with Zinoviev." Continuing, Reingold says: "I can confirm that Zinoviev, Kamenev, Bakayev, Evdokimov, Smirnov, Mrachkovsky, Ter-Vaganyan and Sokolnikov were members of the Trotskyite-Zinovievite centre. Negotiations were carried on about joint activity with the 'Leftists': Shatskin, Lominadze and Sten, and also with the representatives of the Right deviation: Rykov, Bukharin and Tomsky." "The idea of the Zinovievites uniting with the Trotskyites," says Reingold, "arose as far back as 1931. Meeting Zinoviev in his apartment and in his villa that year, I heard him say that it was a pity that we had fallen out with Trotsky." Continuing his testimony, Reingold states that in discussing the general political situation, Zinoviev emphasized that the economic position of the Soviet Union had become stronger and that it was absolutely no use talking about collapse. It was necessary to unite all the forces opposed to the present leadership. That is how the way was paved for a *bloc* with the Trotskyites. The basis for the union of the Trotskyites with the Zinovievites, emphasizes Reingold, was terrorism.

Vyshinsky: How did Zinoviev and Kamenev reconcile terroristic activities with Marxism?

Reingold: In 1932, Zinoviev, at Kamenev's apartment, in the presence of a number of members of the united Trotskyite-Zinovievite centre argued in favor of resorting to terror as follows: although terror is incompatible with Marxism, at the present moment these considerations must be abandoned. There are no other methods available of fighting the leaders of the Party and the Government at the present time. Stalin combines in himself all the strength and firmness of the present Party leadership. Therefore Stalin must be put out of the way in the first place. Kamenev enlarged on this theory and said that the former methods of fighting, namely, attempts to win the masses, combinations with the leaders of the Rightists, and banking on economic difficulties, have failed. That is why the only method of strugge available is terroristic acts against Stalin and his closest comrades-in-arms, Kirov, Voroshilov, Kaganovich, Orjonikidze, Postyshev, Kossior and the others.

"For this purpose," continued Reingold, "it was decided to create an organization of the most carefully chosen and resolute people who could go right through with the job. Simultaneously, negotiations were carried on with the leaders of the Rightists:

Bukharin and Tomsky. After these negotiations Zinoviev definitely said that he had found common political ground with Tomsky in appraising the policy of our country. These conversations continued in 1932 and were carried on between Kamenev, Tomsky and Rykov. Communication with Bukharin was maintained through Karev, an active Zinovievite who was closely connected with the two terroristic groups of Slepkov and Eismont."

Reingold then proceeds to relate his own counter-revolution ary activity which consisted in organizing terrorist groups to assassinate Comrades Stalin and other leaders of the Party and the Government. He enumerates a number of such groups which were directed by Bakayev.

Continuing, Reingold says: "There was an interruption in our terroristic activities between the autumn of 1932 and the summer of 1933 caused by the fact that Zinoviev and Kamenev were compromised in connection with the Ryutin case. In connection with that, in the beginning of 1933, at one of the conferences held in the apartment of Bogdan, Zinoviev's former private secretary, Evdokimov passed on the instruction in the name of the united centre to suspend terroristic work until Zinoviev and Kamenev had returned from exile, until they had declared their repentance, were reinstated in the Party and had gained a certain amount of confidence."

Vyshinsky: Did Evdokimov say that?

Reingold: Evdokimov spoke about that.

Vyshinsky: Did Evdokimov know that Zinoviev and Kamenev were to declare their repentance?

Reingold: He did. He knew that this was in the nature of the Zinovievite organization, which in the past had had no little experience in this sort of repentance.

Reingold goes on to tell the Court about the duplicity which Zinoviev and Kamenev had elevated to a system. Zinoviev and Kamenev, he says, insisted upon every advantage being taken of legal possibilities for the purpose of "crawling on the belly into the Party"—this was Zinoviev's favourite expression—and of winning the confidence of the Party, particularly of Stalin. After this confidence had been restored, strictly secret terroristic work was to be carried on parallel with open work. The combination of these two methods represented the means which, as Zinoviev and Kamenev calculated, could bring them to power. In the event of a success of the terroristic plans, continues Reingold, Zinoviev and Kamenev, having been reinstated in the Party under Stalin, having been forgiven by him, thought they could return to power in the "natural" way.

Vyshinsky: I understand then from what you say that both Kamenev and Zinoviev proceeded along two lines: on the one hand they did all they possibly could to display their loyalty, their devotion to the Party, while on the other hand it was they who were preparing terrorist acts against the leaders of the Party. Is that right?

Reingold: Yes.

Vyshinsky: Accused Zinoviev, Reingold's testimony implicates you in a grave crime. Do you admit your guilt?

Zinoviev: Yes.

Vyshinsky: Accused Kamenev, I put the same question to you.

Kamenev: I answer in the affirmative.

Comrade Vyshinsky reminds Kamenev that he admitted this only after Reingold had given his evidence; that at the preliminary investigation he did not admit this until he had been implicated by others.

Vyshinsky: So you confirm that you had such a monstrous plan?

Kamenev: Yes, there was such a monstrous plan.

Vyshinsky: You worked out this monstrous plan and confirm this now?

Kamenev: Yes, I do.

As a result of the further questioning of Reingold it is ascertained that Kamenev and Zinoviev commissioned Reingold to carry out a number of responsible tasks, in particular, that of creating abroad a special fund for the purpose of financing the terrorist organization in the event of Kamenev and Zinoviev being deported abroad.

Vyshinsky: Accused Kamenev, was there any such talk?

Kamenev: This was in 1929 when I and Zinoviev presumed

that we might be deported abroad like Trotsky and therefore we thought it necessary to create abroad some fund for the purpose of maintaining and continuing the work which we had been carrying on here.

Vyshinsky: From what resources did you think you could set up this fund?

Kamenev: We had certain resources in view.

Vyshinsky: Did you appeal to Reingold for assistance?

Kamenev: Not for assistance. We simply instructed Reingold and Arkus to create this fund. Reingold and Arkus were financial officials under Sokolnikov.

Vyshinsky: Did you propose to organize this fund at the expense of the state?

Kamenev: At any rate not out of Reingold's personal funds.

Vyshinsky: To put it more exactly, you intended to rob the state.

Asked by Comrade Vyshinsky how the Trotskyite-Zinovievite centre had intended to cover up the traces of terroristic crimes, the accused Reingold states that in the event of their coming to power, the Trotskyite-Zinovievite centre intended to kill off all the officials of the G.P.U. who as they supposed might have in their hands threads of the "terroristic conspiracy against the state," and that all their own adherents who were directly and immediately involved in terrorism were likewise to be killed off.

Reingold states: "Zinoviev and Kamenev were both of the opinion, and they told me about this, that on the morrow of the coup d'état, after the seizure of power, Bakayev should be put at the head of the G.P.U. in the capacity of chairman of the G.P.U. By the use of the G.P.U. machinery, he was to assist in covering up the traces, in doing away with, in killing, not only the employees of the People's Commissariat for Internal Affairs—the G.P.U., who might be in possession of any threads of the conspiracy, but also all the direct perpetrators of terroristic acts against Stalin and his immediate assistants. By the hand of Bakayev the Trotskyite-Zinovievite organization was to destroy its own activists, its own terrorist gunmen, who were involved in this matter."

It was also proposed, Reingold continues to testify, that after the seizure of power, Trotsky was to be recalled from abroad and with his support all those who were most devoted to Stalin were to be removed from Party and Soviet posts. Thus it was proposed to seize all power in the country.

Reingold's statements, and also the replies to questions put to Bakayev and Zinoviev by Comrade Vyshinsky, reveal Bakayev in the role of organizer of terrorist groups for which particularly "reliable" persons had been recruited.

Among those "reliable" persons who were named were Bogdan, Zinoviev's former secretary, Radin and Faivilovich, active Zinovievites, and Rumyantsev and Kotolynov, the terrorists, who were executed in connection with the murder of Kirov.

Vyshinsky (to Bakayev): Did Bogdan receive any instructions?

Bakayev: Yes.

Vyshinsky: From whom?

Bakayev: From Zinoviev. On Zinoviev's instructions Bogdan was to shoot Stalin in the Secretariat of the Central Committee.

Vyshinsky: Accused Zinoviev, have you heard Bakayev's testimony?

Zinoviev: It is true that I advised Bakayev to enlist Bogdan for terrorist attempts, and that one of those to be assassinated by him was Stalin.

In this connection Bakayev testifies: "The day after I had been instructed to organize the assassination Zinoviev asked me to come and see him. In his apartment I met Reingold and Bogdan. After greeting me Zinoviev said: 'Here is a gunman for your group; then Reingold recommends also Faivilovich whom I too know as being all right.' "

Vyshinsky: What does it mean "being all right."

Bakayev: An absolutely reliable person.

Vyshinsky: For committing terroristic acts?

Bakayev: Yes.

EXAMINATION OF THE ACCUSED BAKAYEV

Following Reingold, evidence is given by Bakayev. In reply to questions put to him by Comrade Vyshinsky he testifies before the Court how the preparations for these terroristic acts were carried on. Particularly intense terroristic activity was carried on in August 1932 and in the autumn of 1934. Bakayev mentions the names of those who took part in the preparation of terroristic acts. These were Reingold, Pickel, Faivilovich, Radin, and others.

Bakayev testifies before the Court how the terrorists of the Trotskyite-Zinovievite centre tried to destroy all clues and preserve secrecy. In the autumn of 1932 Zinoviev and Kamenev were expelled from the Party. The question then arose: What to do next? Then Bakayev met Zinoviev, Evdokimov, Kuklin, Sharov, Dreitzer and others and it was resolved to suspend terroristic activities for a time. In the autumn of 1934 they were resumed.

Bakayev testifies that in October 1934 an attempt on the life of Stalin was organized in Moscow under the direction of Kamenev, Evdokimov and himself, in which he, Bakayev, took a direct part. The attempt failed. When the attempt failed Bakayev went to Kamenev and told him about it.

Continuing his testimony, Bakayev says: "Kamenev said: 'A pity, let's hope that next time we'll be more successful.' Then turning to Evdokimov he asked how things were in Leningrad. Evdokimov replied that it would he advisable to check up on the situation in Leningrad and that Bakayev should be sent to Leningrad. Kamenev agreed—yes, he said, Bakayev absolutely must go. I agreed to go. Before my departure I asked Evdokimov whom I was to report to there and with whom I was to talk. Evdokimov replied that I was to report to Levin. I said that I did not know Levin's address as I had not seen him for many years. Evdokimov promised to arrange for Levin or Mandelstamm to meet me at the station. I went and was actually met at the station by Levin who said: 'So Gregory Evseyevich (Zinoviev) doesn't trust either Gertik, Kuklin or even Evdokimov, but sends people here to check up on our mood and our work. Well, we're not a proud lot' . . . I asked him to call the boys together. Shortly after, in addition to Levin and Mandelstamm, Sossitsky, Vladimir Rumyantsev, Kotolynov and Myasnikov gathered together in Levin's apartment. Kotolynov said that he had established a regular watch over Kirov and that Kirov was so well covered that there would be no difficulty in killing him. I asked to be introduced to one of those who had been assigned to commit terroristic acts. Levin asked Kotolynov to invite Leonid Nikolayev. I knew that Leonid Nikolayev was a member of the Leningrad organization. Levin said that Nikolayev was an old member of the Young Communist League whom Evdokimov had known for many years and whom he had given the best recommendation as an absolutely reliable person. Nikolayev gave me the impression of being a determined and convinced terrorist. He told me that he had succeeded in finding out the exact time when Kirov travelled from his apartment to the Smolny, that he could kill Kirov either near the Smolny or in the Smolny itself and that he had tried to get an appointment with Kirov so as to shoot him but had failed to get an appointment. Nikolayev further reported that he, together with two other terrorists, were keeping a watch on Kirov."

In his testimony Bakayev says that of all the activities of the terrorist centre he was only aware of the decision to assassinate Stalin and Kirov, and that he only learned of preparations having been made for other terroristic acts when he read the indictment.

Vyshinsky: Bakayev, is it correct that you were a member of the terrorist centre?

Bakayev: Yes, it is.

Vyshinsky: In 1932 you received instructions to organize the assassination of Comrade Stalin. Was that so?

Bakayev: Yes.

Vyshinsky: Did you take a number of practical measures to carry out these instructions, namely, to organize several attempts on the life of Comrade Stalin, which failed through no fault of yours?

Bakayev: That is so.

Vyshinsky: Besides, did you take part in the assassination of Comrade Kirov?

Bakayev: Yes.

Vyshinsky: Besides, did you go to Leningrad on the instructions of the terrorist centre, to check up on the preparations that were being made for this assassination?

Bakayev: Yes.

Vyshinsky: On your return from Leningrad, you reported that everything was in order, that the preparations for the murder were proceeding successfully. While you were in Leningrad did you meet Kotolynov, Rumyantsev and others?

Bakayev: Yes.

Vyshinsky: In addition, did you meet Nikolayev, give him instructions about the assassination and convince yourself that Nikolayev was a man of determination and could carry out the instructions given?

Bakayev: Yes.

Questioned further, however, Bakayev tried to minimize the part he had played considering that he was merely a "co-organizer" of the preparations for the foul murder of Comrade S. M. Kirov.

Vyshinsky: You gave the signals, you checked up on the time, you checked up on all that was being done at your signal, you perpetrated a deed—doesn't that mean being the organizer of the crime?

Bakayev: Yes, that means being the organizer of the crime.

Vyshinsky: So we are correct in saying that you were the organizer of the assassination of Kirov?

Bakayev: Well, yes, but I was not the only one.

Vyshinsky: You were not the only one, Evdokimov was with you. Accused Zinoviev, you too were an organizer of the assassination of Comrade Kirov, weren't you?

Zinoviev: I think Bakayev is right when he says that the real and principal culprits of the foul murder of Kirov were myself, Trotsky and Kamenev who organized the united terrorist centre. Bakayev played an important, but not the decisive part in it.

Vyshinsky: The decisive part was played by you, Trotsky and Kamenev. Accused Kamenev, do you associate yourself with Zinoviev's statement that the principal organizers were you, Trotsky and Zinoviev, and that Bakayev played the part of a practical organizer?

Kamenev: Yes.

EXAMINATION OF THE ACCUSED PICKEL

The Supreme Court then proceeds to examine the accused Pickel. Pickel was one of Zinoviev's most trusted men and for many years was in charge of his secretariat. He admits that as an active member of the Moscow terrorist centre he was aware of all the principal decisions and terroristic measures of the united centre. In the autumn of 1932 Pickel joined the fighting terrorist organization of which Bakayev was the leader, and agreed to take part in the attempt on the life of Comrade Stalin. Pickel corrobor-ates the testimony given by Reingold and Bakayev that Zinoviev directly guided the preparations for this attempt. He gives a striking characterization of the principal leaders of this terroristic activity, including Zinoviev, who were masters in the art of playing upon the ambitions, on the particularities of each of their accomplices. To rouse passion, to rouse hatred, to rouse their supporters to the boiling point, this, according to Pickel, was the only art of which the heads of the counter-revolutionary, Trotskyite-Zinovievite terrorist *bloc,* were masters.

Pickel, supplementing Bakayev's testimony, states that in the autumn of 1933 Bogdan made another attempt on the life of Comrade Stalin. In this connection Pickel depicts the atmosphere that prevailed in the terrorist centre, the members of which did not hesitate to resort to the most sordid methods to wipe out the traces of their criminal activities.

Pickel admits that Bogdan's suicide was in fact murder by decision of the terrorist centre. In this crime a particularly active part was played by Bakayev. Bakayev spent the whole night with Bogdan before the latter committed suicide and persuaded him either to make an attempt on Stalin's life or to commit suicide. Bogdan took his own life and, as he had been instructed, left a note making it appear that he was the victim of the Party cleansing.

Pickel goes on to relate what preparations were made for a terroristic act against Comrade Stalin in 1934. Pickel's part in this was that he put Bakayev in touch with Radin whom Pickel prepared for the carrying out of his terroristic act.

Another very characteristic touch, indicating how the Trotskyites and Zinovievites tried to wipe out all traces and save their terrorist organization, was Pickel's admission that in order to avert the discovery and break-up of the organization, he was told in 1934 to go to a remote place for a time. Being a member of the

AUGUST 20 (MORNING SESSION)

EXAMINATION OF THE ACCUSED KAMENEV

The morning session of August 20 commences with the examination of the accused L. B. Kamenev.

Kamenev states: "The terrorist conspiracy was organized and guided by myself, Zinoviev and Trotsky. I became convinced that the policy of the Party, the policy of its leadership, had been victorious in the only sense in which the political victory in the land of socialism is possible, that this policy was recognized by the masses of the toilers. Our banking on the possibility of a split in the Party also proved groundless. We counted on the Rightist group of Rykov, Bukharin and Tomsky. The removal of this group from the leadership and the fact that it had become discredited in the eyes of the toiling masses deprived us of this trump card as well. It was no use counting on any kind of serious internal difficulties to secure the overthrow of the leadership which had guided the country through extremely difficult stages, through industrialization and collectivization. Two paths remained: either honestly and completely to put a stop to the struggle against the Party, or to continue this struggle, but without any hope of obtaining any mass support whatsoever, without a political platform, without a banner, that is to say, by means of individual terror. We chose the second path. In this we were guided by our boundless hatred of the leaders of the Party and the country, and by a thirst for power with which we were once so closely associated and from which we were cast aside by the course of historical development."

Replying to Comrade Vyshinsky, the accused Kamenev relates to the Court how the Zinovievites entered into a *bloc* with the Trotskyites for the purpose of organizing a terroristic struggle against the Party and the Soviet state

"We carried on negotiations about the *bloc* with Smirnov, Mrachkovsky and Ter-Vaganyan, not as with men who independently issued political instructions," says Kamenev. "They were of value to us as men who precisely repeated the instructions of Trotsky. Knowing Smirnov and Mrachkovsky as active Trotskyites, knowing that Smirnov had been abroad and had established contact with Trotsky there, we were absolutely sure that the instructions concerning terrorism conveyed by Smirnov and Mrachkovsky, and supported by them, were the exact instructions of Trotsky. It was on this basis, and because Trotsky's instructions on terror coincided with our own inclinations, that we concluded what is here called a '*bloc*,' and what should be called a narrow terrorist conspiracy. This conspiracy took shape in 1932 as an organizational union which had no platform at all, and which set itself the aim of seizing power by disorganizing the government by terroristic means, by eliminating and assassinating Stalin, as the leader of the Party and the country, as well as his nearest comrades-in-arms."

The accused Kamenev fully confirms the leading part played by I. N. Smirnov in the Trotskyite part of the terrorist Trotskyite-Zinovievite centre, and concerning Smirnov's denials he says: "It is ridiculous wriggling, which only creates a comical impression."

Kamenev then goes on to tell the Court about the practical activities of the counter-revolutionary terrorists. He says:

"In the summer of 1932 a meeting of our Zinovievite centre was held in our villa in Ilyinskoye. I myself, Zinoviev, Evdokimov, Bakayev, Kuklin and Karev were present. At this meeting Zinoviev reported that the union with the Trotskyites, who had received Trotsky's personal instructions to commit terroristic acts, was an accomplished fact. At this very meeting Bakayev was instructed to carry out a terroristic act in Moscow, and Karev in Leningrad. The exile of myself and Zinoviev somewhat held up the execution of our terroristic plans. When we returned to Moscow, we made no changes whatever in the basis of our *bloc*. On the contrary, we proceeded to press forward the terroristic conspiracy. This pressing forward was caused by two circumstances: first, the collapse of the policy of double-dealing pursued by Zinoviev, who was removed from the editorial board of the *Bolshevik*. This made us fear that information about our connection with Trotsky might have reached the Party leadership. Secondly, the Trotskyites energetically insisted on expediting the terroristic activities, having received instructions to this effect from Trotsky. Organizationally, this found expression in the decision that was adopted to hasten the assassination of Stalin and the assassination of Kirov."

Continuing, the accused Kamenev testifies: "In June 1934 I myself went to Leningrad where I instructed the active Zinovievite Yakovlev to prepare an attempt on the life of Kirov parallel with the Nikolayev-Kotolynov group. In the beginning of November 1934 I learned from Bakayev's report all the details of the preparations that were being made by the Nikolayev group to assassinate Kirov."

Vyshinsky: Was Kirov's assassination directly the work of your hands?

Kamenev: Yes.

Kamenev gives the following testimony on the composition of the terrorist Trotskyite-Zinovievite centre:

"The centre of the conspiracy consisted of the following persons: myself, Zinoviev, Evdokimov, Bakayev and Kuklin, on behalf of the Zinovievites; Smirnov, Mrachkovsky and Ter-Vaganyan on behalf of the Trotskyites. Among the leaders of the conspiracy another person may be named who in point of fact was one of the leaders, but who, in view of the special plans we made in regard to him, was not drawn into the practical work. I refer to Sokolnikov.

Vyshinsky: Who was a member of the centre, but whose part was kept a strict secret?

Kamenev: Yes.

Continuing, Kamenev says: "Knowing that we might be discovered, we designated a small group to continue our terroristic activities. For this purpose we designated Sokolnikov. It seemed to us that on the side of the Trotskyites this role could be successfully performed by Serebryakov and Radek. Asked about this, Mrachkovsky said: Yes, in our opinion Serebryakov and Radek could act as substitutes if, contrary to our expectations, our leading group should be discovered."

Kamenev goes on to say that the Zinovievites carried on negotiations and established contact with other counter-revolutionary groups as well.

"In 1932," he says, "I personally conducted negotiations with the so-called 'Leftist' group of Lominadze and Shatsky. In this group I found enemies of the Party leadership quite prepared to resort to the most determined measures of struggle against it. At the same time, I myself and Zinoviev maintained constant contact with the former 'Workers' Opposition' group of Shlyapnikov and Medvedyev. In 1932, 1933 and 1934 I personally maintained relations with Tomsky and Bukharin and sounded their political sentiments. They sympathized with us. When I asked Tomsky about Rykov's frame of mind, he replied: 'Rykov thinks the same as I do.' In reply to my question as to what Bukharin thought, he said: 'Bukharin thinks the same as I do, but is pursuing somewhat different tactics: he does not agree with the line of the Party, but is pursuing tactics of persistently enrooting himself in the Party and winning the personal confidence of the leadership.' "

In examining the accused Kamenev the Court deals in detail with the double-dealing to which the conspirators resorted in addition to terrorism in their fight against the Party.

Vyshinsky: What appraisal should be given of the articles and statements you wrote in 1933, in which you expressed loyalty to the Party? Deception?

Kamenev: No, worse than deception.

Vyshinsky: Perfidy?

Kamenev: Worse.

Vyshinsky: Worse than deception, worse than perfidy—find the word. Treason?

Kamenev: You have found it.

Vyshinsky: Accused Zinoviev, do you confirm this?

Zinoviev: Yes.

Vyshinsky: Treason, perfidy, double-dealing?

Zinoviev: Yes.

Proceeding to explain the motives of his conduct, the accused Kamenev declares:

"I can admit only one thing: that having set ourselves the monstrously criminal aim of disorganizing the government of the land of socialism, we resorted to methods of struggle which in our

68

opinion suited this aim and which are as low and as vile as the aim which we set before ourselves."

In the further process of the examination the accused Kamenev still more clearly and definitely speaks of that which guided the Zinovievites in their activities.

Vyshinsky: Consequently, your struggle against the leaders of the Party and the government was guided by motives of a personal base character—by the thirst for personal power?

Kamenev: Yes, by the thirst for power of our group.

Vyshinsky: Don't you think that this has nothing in common with social ideals?

Kamenev: It has as much in common as revolution has with counter-revolution.

Vyshinsky: That is, you are on the side of counter-revolution?

Kamenev: Yes.

Vyshinsky: Consequently, you clearly perceive that you are fighting against socialism?

Kamenev: We clearly perceive that we are fighting against the leaders of the Party and of the government who are leading the country to socialism.

Vyshinsky: Thereby you are fighting socialism as well, aren't you?

Kamenev: You are drawing the conclusion of an historian and prosecutor.

At the end of the examination of the accused Kamenev, Comrade Vyshinsky reminds him that in his testimony on August 10 he stated that the conspirators intended, after seizing power, to appoint Bakayev chief of the O.G.P.U. and so cover up the traces of their crimes.

Kamenev asserts that the Trotskyite-Zinovievite centre had in this connection not the intention of physically exterminating those who directly committed terroristic acts, but of diverting the investigation of terroristic acts into false channels.

The accused Reingold categorically asserts that the Trotskyite-Zinovievite centre intended to wipe out their gunmen terrorists in order to shield the Trotskyite-Zinovievite leaders and cover up the traces of the crimes. Indignant at Kamenev's statement, Reingold says:

"Let Kamenev not pretend that he is such an innocent creature. He is a hardened politician who would force his way to power over mountains of corpses. Would he hesitate to kill off one or two terrorists? No one will believe him!"

EXAMINATION OF THE WITNESS YAKOVLEV

The Court then proceeds to examine the witness Yakovlev, summoned at the request of the State Prosecutor.

Comrade Vyshinsky asks Yakovlev to tell about Kamenev's connections with him, Yakovlev, in the terroristic activities pursued by Kamenev.

Yakovlev testifies that Karev, who worked with him in the counter-revolutionary group at the Academy of Sciences, had informed him of the following: In the autumn of 1932 the Zinovievites organized a *bloc* with the Trotskyites. A united Trotskyite-Zinovievite centre was set up. The principal method of fighting against the Party and the Soviet government adopted by this centre was terrorism, which it was decided to direct against the leaders of the Party and the government, in the first place against Stalin and Kirov.

Continuing, Yakovlev says: "This was confirmed by Kamenev himself in a conversation with me in 1934. In this connection Kamenev commissioned me to organize a terrorist group at the Academy of Sciences. I accepted this commission. At the same time Kamenev informed me that instructions to prepare terroristic acts had been given also to other groups. In Moscow, preparations were being made for an attempt on the life of Stalin, and in Leningrad it was proposed to commit a terroristic act against Kirov, this mission being entrusted to the Rumyantsev-Kotolynov group."

Vyshinsky: In his testimony the accused Kamenev mentioned Yakovlev (turning to Kamenev). Is this the Yakovlev in question?

Kamenev: Yes, it is.

Vyshinsky: And did you meet him?

Kamenev: I did.

Vyshinsky: Did you entrust him with the task of preparing a terroristic act parallel with that of the Rumyantsev-Kotolynov group? Do you confirm this?

Kamenev: Yes.

Vyshinsky: And you, Yakovlev, do you confirm this?

Yakovlev: Yes.

After several questions have been put to Kamenev by Ter-Vaganyan and Smirnov which elicited the fact that Kamenev had repeated conversations about terrorism with Ter-Vaganyan in 1932, the Court proceeds to examine the accused Zinoviev.

EXAMINATION OF THE ACCUSED ZINOVIEV

Zinoviev begins his testimony by relating the history of the restoration of the united Trotskyite-Zinovievite centre in 1932. He emphasizes that there never were any material differences between the Trotskyites and the Zinovievites.

"Our differences with Trotsky after the Fifteenth Congress," says Zinoviev, "when Trotsky used the word 'treachery' in relation to me and Kamenev, were really slight zig-zags, petty disagreements. We committed no treachery whatever against Trotsky at that time, but committed one more act of treachery against the Bolshevik Party to which we belonged."

But it was precisely at that moment, says Zinoviev, continuing his testimony, that we were completely adopting, as our main line, double-dealing to which we had already resorted previously, which we had practised in 1926 and in 1927. In 1928, however, after the Fifteenth Congress of the C.P.S.U., we could not take a single step, we could not utter a single word without betraying the Party in one way or another, without resorting to double-dealing in one way or another. "From 1928 to 1932," Zinoviev says further, "there was not for one moment any real difference between ourselves and the Trotskyites. And so the logic of things carried us to terrorism.

"We banked on a growth of difficulties. We hoped that they would grow to such an extent that we and the Rightists and the Trotskyites, and the smaller groups associated with them, could come out openly. We dreamt of coming out in a united front. At that time we thought that the Rightists had most chances of success, that their prognoses were more likely to come true, and that their names would have particular power of attraction. At that time we attempted to place particular emphasis on our closeness to them."

Continuing, Zinoviev says: "At the same time certain underground groups of the Right as well as of the so-called 'Left' trend, sought contact with me and Kamenev. Approaches were

71

made by the remnants of the 'Workers' Opposition': by Shlyapnikov and Medvedyev. Approaches came from the groups of the so-called 'Leftists': that is, Lominadze, Shatskin, Sten and others. Approaches also came from the so-called 'individuals,' to whose numbers belonged Smilga, and to a certain extent, Sokolnikov."

Zinoviev further says: "In the second half of 1932 we realized that our banking on a growth of difficulties in the country had failed. We began to realize that the Party and its Central Committee would overcome these difficulties. But both in the first and in the second half of 1932 we were filled with hatred towards the Central Committee of the Party and towards Stalin."

Continuing, Zinoviev says: "We were convinced that the leadership must be superseded at all costs, that it must be superseded by us, along with Trotsky. In this situation I had meetings with Smirnov who has accused me here of frequently telling untruths. Yes, I often told untruths. I started doing that from the moment I began fighting the Bolshevik Party. In so far as Smirnov took the road of fighting the Party, he too is telling untruths. But it seems, the difference between him and myself is that I have decided firmly and irrevocably to tell at this last moment the truth, whereas, he it seems has adopted a different decision.

Vyshinsky: Are you telling the whole truth now?

Zinoviev: Now I am telling the whole truth to the end.

Vyshinsky: Remember that on January 15-16, 1935, at the sessions of the Military Collegium of the Supreme Court, you also asserted that you were telling the whole truth.

Zinoviev: Yes. On January 15-16 I did not tell the whole truth.

Vyshinsky: You did not tell the truth, but you maintained that you were telling the truth.

Continuing his testimony, Zinoviev relates that during his conversations with Smirnov in 1931 he conferred with him with regard to an understanding on uniting the Trotskyites and the Zinovievites on the basis of terrorism and that this was done on Trotsky's instruction. "I. N. Smirnov entirely agreed with this instruction, and carried it out wholeheartedly and with conviction," testifies Zinoviev. "I spoke a great deal with Smirnov about choosing people for terroristic activities and also designated the persons against whom the weapon of terrorism was to be directed. The name of Stalin was mentioned in the first place, followed by those of Kirov, Voroshilov and other leaders of the Party and the government. For the purpose of executing these plans, a Trotskyite-Zinovievite terrorist centre was formed, the leading part in which was played by myself—Zinoviev, and by Smirnov on behalf of the Trotskyites."

Vyshinsky: Thus, summing up your testimony, we may draw the conclusion that in the organization of the Trotskyite-Zinovievite terrorist *bloc* and centre, the decisive part was played, on the one hand, by you, as the leader of the Zinovievites, and, on the other, by Trotsky through his representatives?

Zinoviev: That is correct.

Vyshinsky: At that time Trotsky's principal representative and even deputy in the U.S.S.R. was I. N. Smirnov?

Zinoviev: That is correct.

Vyshinsky: Was the recognition of the necessity of terrorism the decisive condition for uniting the Trotskyites and Zinovievites?

Zinoviev: Yes.

Vyshinsky: Did you and Smirnov designate the persons against whom terror was to be directed in the first instance? Is it true that these persons were Comrade Stalin, Comrade Kirov and Comrade Voroshilov?

Zinoviev: That was the central question.

Continuing his testimony Zinoviev states, in reply to a question by Comrade Vyshinsky as to what practical steps were taken in preparation for the assassination of the leaders of the Party and the government, that in the autumn of 1932 a conference was held in Ilyinskoye attended by himself, Kamenev, Evdokimov, Bakayev and Karev. At this conference Bakayev was entrusted with the practical direction of matters connected with terrorism.

Continuing, Zinoviev says: "When Kamenev and I went into exile after the Ryutin affair fell through, we left Evdokimov, Bakayev and Smirnov in charge of terroristic activities. We placed special hopes on Smirnov." "At the same time," says Zinoviev, "I conducted negotiations with Tomsky, whom I informed about our *bloc* with the Trotskyites. Tomsky expressed complete solidarity with us. After our return from exile the first steps we took were directed toward liquidating, if one may so express it, the breakdown of our terroristic activities, the fiasco of the conspirators, and

73

toward restoring confidence in order to be able to continue our terroristic activities later on. We continued our tactics, which represented a combination of ever subtler forms of perfidious double-dealing with the preparation of the conspiracy."

"After the murder of Sergei Mironovich Kirov," says Zinoviev, "our perfidy went to such lengths that I sent an obituary about Kirov to *Pravda*. That obituary was not published. As far as I remember, Kamenev, and I think Evdokimov also, wrote obituaries on Kirov. At all events, Kamenev knew that I would send in my obituary.

Vyshinsky: Then you did that by preliminary arrangement?

Zinoviev: As far as I remember, I told Kamenev that I was sending in an obituary. He, I think, said that he would either send one himself or that the office at which he was working would send a collective obituary which he would sign.

Vyshinsky: Don't you recall this, accused Kamenev?

Kamenev: I do not remember. And I did not know that Zinoviev intended to send in an obituary. I knew that after the events of December 1, and after the arrest of Bakayev and Evdokimov, Zinoviev came to me and showed me the draft of a letter addressed to Yagoda, General Commissar of State Security, in which he stated that he was disturbed by these arrests and asked to be summoned in order to establish the fact that he, Zinoviev, had nothing to do with this murder.

Vyshinsky: Was that the case, accused Zinoviev?

Zinoviev: Yes, it was.

Kamenev: Then I said that he should not do that because I thought that after all we had done we ought to keep some composure.

Vyshinsky: Did you succeed in keeping your composure?

Kamenev: Yes, I wrote no such letter.

After that, Zinoviev states, he sent Bakayev in 1934 to Leningrad to investigate the progress reached in the preparations for the assassination of Kirov. Zinoviev says: "I sent Bakayev to Leningrad as one who enjoyed our confidence, who knew very well the personnel of the terrorists, in order to check up on the people, the situation, the degree of preparedness, etc. On his return from Leningrad Bakayev reported that everything was in order."

Vyshinsky: Were you sure that everything was going on well?

Zinoviev: I considered that all the work had been done.

Vyshinsky: Did you hasten, did you expedite the assassination of Kirov? Were there times when you expressed dissatisfaction with a certain measure of slowness on the part of your terrorists?

Zinoviev: Yes, I expressed some dissatisfaction.

Vyshinsky: Can we say that you were not only the organizer and inspirer of the assassination of Kirov, but also the organizer of the more expeditious realization of this event?

Zinoviev: There was a time when I tried to expedite it.

Continuing his testimony, Zinoviev speaks of his meetings with M. Lurye (Emel) who had brought Trotsky's terrorist instructions. "I knew," Zinoviev says, "that M. Lurye was a Trotskyite, and not a Trotskyite only, for when he spoke one could even hear the language of a fascist."

Vyshinsky: In what did his fascism show itself?

Zinoviev: His fascism showed itself when he said that in a situation like the present we must resort to the use of every possible means.

From a reply to a question put by Comrade Vyshinsky to M. Lurye it becomes clear that Zinoviev met M. Lurye three times after the latter's arrival from Berlin. At one meeting between M. Lurye and Zinoviev, at the latter's apartment, the conversation between the two was frank. They discussed the terrorist instructions of Trotsky which M. Lurye had received in Berlin through Ruth Fischer and Maslov, and which he then conveyed to Zinoviev through Herzberg.

M. Lurye says: "I asked Zinoviev whether he was informed about the case of Nathan Lurye. Zinoviev replied in the affirmative."

Further, M. Lurye told Zinoviev that Nathan Lurye was connected with a certain Franz Weitz. When Zinoviev asked who Franz Weitz was, M. Lurye informed him that Franz Weitz was a man particularly trusted by Himmler, the present chief of the Gestapo. "I again asked him," continues M. Lurye, "whether he was posted on this group. Zinoviev replied in the affirmative. To my perplexed question as to whether it was permissible for Marxists to practise individual terror and maintain contact with fascist groups, followed the reply, 'You are an historian, aren't you, Moissei Ilyich,' and he drew the parallel of Bismarck and Lassalle, add- ing: 'why cannot we today utilize Himmler?' "

After Lurye's replies Zinoviev asserts that this sentence was uttered by Lurye himself. He admits however that Lurye ac- tually visited him in his apartment and discussed terrorism with him.

Replying to a question put to him by Comrade Ulrich, President of the Court, about the part he, Zinoviev, played in preparing a terroristic act against Comrade Stalin, Zinoviev says that he took part in this affair and that he knew of two attempts on the life of Comrade Stalin in which Reingold, Dreitzer and Pickel had taken part. Zinoviev also confirms that he recommended his private sec- retary, Bogdan, to Bakayev, the leader of the terrorist groups, as the one to assassinate Comrade Stalin.

Vyshinsky: Did you recommend Bogdan to Bakayev for the purpose of carrying out the assassination of Comrade Stalin? Do you confirm that?

Zinoviev: I do.

EXAMINATION OF THE WITNESS SAFONOVA

The court then proceeds to examine the witness Safonova, whose case has been set aside for separate trial and who was sum- moned at the request of the State Prosecutor.

Safonova testifies that she was a member of the Trotsky- ite centre and took an active part in the work of that centre. She goes on to say that in 1931 I. N. Smirnov informed the centre of the Trotskyite organization, in the persons of Ter-Va- ganyan, Mrachkovsky and herself, that he had received in Ber- lin, through Sedov, instructions to adopt terroristic methods of struggle. I. N. Smirnov, in conveying these instructions, emphasized that they came from Trotsky. Safonova further testifies: "At that same meeting Smirnov informed us that the centre had decided to adopt terrorism, and in the first place to commit a terroristic act against Stalin. In 1932 Smirnov received from Trotsky directions brought by Gaven. These directions were a direct confirmation of Trotsky's instruction on terrorism previously received by Smirnov through Sedov. Smirnov also informed us about these directions. These directions were not only a confirmation of those conveyed through Sedov, but were at the same time instructions on the necessity of hastening the terroristic act against Stalin."

Safonova cites another fact illustrating I. N. Smirnov's attitude towards terrorism. "One day," she says, "Mrachkovsky, on returning from an official visit to Stalin, related his conversation with Stalin. I myself and I. N. Smirnov were present. In relating his conversation with Stalin, Mrachkovsky linked up his story with the prospects of our further struggle and declared that the only way out was to assassinate Stalin. I. N. Smirnov strongly backed Mrachkovsky's conclusion.

"Before my departure for the Amur-Baikal railway construction job in December 1932," says Safonova, continuing her evidence, "I had a conversation with Smirnov about the further work of our organization in connection with the decision on terrorism which had been adopted. I. N. Smirnov categorically confirmed that Stalin must be assassinated, that Stalin would be assassinated."

Smirnov denies that he had passed on to Ter-Vaganyan, Mrachkovsky and Safonova Trotsky's instruction to adopt terrorism. He also denies that, when Mrachkovsky returned after his talk with Stalin, he spoke of the necessity of assassinating Stalin. However, replies to questions put by Comrade Vyshinsky to Ter-Vaganyan, Safonova and Mrachkovsky establish that this actually did take place.

In view of the fact that Safonova's evidence completely exposed Smirnov, Comrade Vyshinsky makes clear the relations between Smirnov and Safonova.

Vyshinsky: What were your relations with Safonova?

Smirnov: Good.

Vyshinsky: And more?

Smirnov: We were intimately related.

Vyshinsky: You were husband and wife?

Smirnov: Yes.

Vyshinsky: No personal grudges between you?

AUGUST 20 (EVENING SESSION)

EXAMINATION OF THE ACCUSED I. N. SMIRNOV

A great part of the evening session is taken up by the examination of the accused I. N. Smirnov.

I. N. Smirnov was one of the leaders of the Trotskyite organization since its formation, the closest friend of Trotsky and the actual organizer and leader of the underground Trotskyite counter-revolutionary activities in the U.S.S.R., who maintained personal connections with Trotsky and the Trotskyite organizations abroad.

Smirnov, Trotsky's deputy in the U.S.S.R., as the accused have defined him, and the leader of the Trotskyite centre, denies his own direct part in the terroristic activities and only partly admits his crimes.

In May 1931 Smirnov went abroad on an official business trip. In Berlin he met Sedov, Trotsky's son and agent. Smirnov claims that this was an "accidental" meeting. During his "accidental" meeting, Smirnov hastened to make arrangements with Sedov about their next meeting which took place in Smirnov's lodgings. Sedov told Smirnov that it was necessary to change the old methods of struggle against the Party, and that the time had arrived to adopt terroristic methods of struggle. Smirnov tries to make it appear that this was Sedov's own opinion with which he, Smirnov, allegedly did not agree. Nevertheless, Smirnov right there promised Sedov to establish communications with him, and to establish "informational" communications with Trotsky. Smirnov received from Sedov two addresses for correspondence and agreed with him upon a password for sending agents. On his return to Moscow, Smirnov immediately informed his associates of his conversation with Sedov regarding terrorism.

Vyshinsky: Although you were not in agreement with Sedov, you nevertheless thought it necessary to inform your underground organization about this terroristic line?

Smirnov: Yes, I did not anticipate that they would take this information as Trotsky's directions.

This assertion, however, is refuted by the testimony of the accused Mrachkovsky, whom Smirnov had informed that in Berlin he had established contact, through Sedov, with Trotsky from whom the directions on terrorism had originated.

Vyshinsky: When Smirnov told you about his conversation with Sedov, you understood the contents of the conversation to be not mere information but instructions?

Mrachkovsky: Yes.

Vyshinsky: What did those instructions say?

Mrachkovsky: They said that the instructions which had existed up to that time, that is up to 1931, had become obsolete. Trotsky proposed that another method, a sharper method, be adopted.

Vyshinsky: Who proposed, Sedov or Trotsky?

Mrachkovsky: Trotsky.

Vyshinsky: Did Smirnov speak about Trotsky?

Mrachkovsky: Yes, he spoke about Trotsky, since Sedov was no authority either for him or for us.

Vyshinsky: Accused Smirnov, is it true that Sedov was not an authority for you?

Smirnov: No, Sedov was not an authority for me.

The accused Smirnov tries at first to assert that in 1931 and in 1932 Trotsky was no authority for him either. However he immediately admits that in 1932 he received through Yuri Gaven instructions from Trotsky urging the adoption of terrorism against the leaders of the Party and the government; he accepted these instructions for the purpose of carrying them out, and communicated them to the centre.

Vyshinsky: Was the centre organized on the basis of terrorism?

Smirnov: Yes.

Vyshinsky: Were you a member of that centre?

Smirnov: Yes, I was.

Vyshinsky: Consequently, those instructions were meant for you too?

Smirnov: Yes, they were communicated to me.

Vyshinsky: They were not only communicated through you, but were also instructions for you?

Smirnov: They were forwarded as instructions.

Vyshinsky: Did you accept them?

Smirnov: Yes.

Vyshinsky: How can you maintain, then, that Trotsky, from whom these instructions orginated, was not an authority for you?

Smirnov tries to reduce his own part to that of merely communicating Trotsky's instructions to the centre; he tries to evade responsibility for the work of the centre.

Smirnov: I listened to those instructions and communicated them to the centre. The centre accepted them, but I did not take part in its work.

Vyshinsky: So when did you leave the centre?

Smirnov: I did not intend to resign; there was nothing to resign from.

Vyshinsky: Did the centre exist?

Smirnov: What sort of a centre. . . .

Vyshinsky: Mrachkovsky, did the centre exist?

Mrachkovsky: Yes.

Vyshinsky: Zinoviev, did the centre exist?

Zinoviev: Yes.

Vyshinsky: Evdokimov, did the centre exist?

Evdokimov: Yes.

Vyshinsky: Bakayev, did the centre exist?

Bakayev: Yes.

Vyshinsky: How, then, Smirnov, can you take the liberty to maintain that no centre existed?

Smirnov once again refers to the absence of meetings of the centre, but the testimony of Zinoviev, Ter-Vaganyan and Mrachkovsky again proves him to be lying. In reply to questions put to him by the State Prosecutor, Zinoviev confirms the fact that he was in continuous communication with Smirnov. Ter-Vaganyan confirms the role Smirnov played as the leader of the Trotskyite part of the *bloc,* who worked to organize, consolidate and unite the two parts of the *bloc.* Mrachkovsky says: "Smirnov is trying to pass

81

as a simple village postman, but we regarded Smirnov as Trotsky's deputy."

In connection with Smirnov's testimony, the accused Olberg informs the Court of his repeated meetings with Sedov, Trotsky's son, in Berlin, in 1931. At one of these meetings, in November-December 1931, Sedov informed Olberg of his meeting with I. N. Smirnov. Sedov spoke with great respect of Smirnov, as the leader of the Trotskyite organization in the U.S.S.R. He said that he, Sedov, had communicated to Smirnov Trotsky's instructions on the necessity to embark upon terroristic activities. Olberg further states that he and the other Trotskyites abroad and in the Soviet Union regarded Sedov solely as a vehicle for transmitting the will, the tasks and the policy of Trotsky.

The further examination of Smirnov confirms that the accused received and passed on additional instructions from Trotsky on terrorism.

Vyshinsky: It can be considered as established that in 1932 you received fresh instructions from Trotsky through Gaven?

Smirnov: Yes.

Vyshinsky: Did these instructions contain direct reference to the necessity of embarking on a terroristic struggle against the leadership of the Party?

Smirnov: Quite true.

Vyshinsky: In the first place, against whom?

Smirnov: No names were mentioned there.

Vyshinsky: But you understood that the terroristic struggle was to begin first against Comrade Stalin?

Smirnov: Yes, I understood it to mean that.

Vyshinsky: And that is what you communicated to your colleagues?

Smirnov: Yes.

The accused persists in his evasions and tries to deny the part he played as the leader of the Trotskyite organization. The Court investigation deals in detail with this question. The examination of the accused elicits the fact that it was on the direct instructions of Smirnov that Ter-Vaganyan negotiated with the Zinovievites about the *bloc*. It becomes clear that Mrachkovsky trained terrorist groups on the direct instructions of Smirnov. It is confirmed that neither Ter-Vaganyan nor Mrachkovsky gave any instructions to Smirnov, but themselves received instructions from him. And finally, the fact is elicited that direct communication with Trotsky was maintained personally by Smirnov right up to his arrest. Under the weight of all these irrefutable facts Smirnov at last admits that it was he and no one else who was the head of the Trotskyite organization.

But the accused makes this confession only after the prosecution has exposed him by absolutely incontrovertible facts.

Desiring to cover up the traces of his activities in organizing the terrorist Trotskyite-Zinovievite *bloc*, Smirnov tries to invent a new version saying that the *bloc* was organized without his direct participation. From the testimony of the accused it appears however that the formation of the *bloc* was the result of direct negotiations between Smirnov and Zinoviev, Kamenev and Ter-Vaganyan, Evdokimov and Mrachkovsky, and that these negotiations for the organization of the *bloc* were conducted on the basis of the first instructions on terror received by Smirnov from Trotsky through Sedov in 1931.

The State Prosecutor then inquires into Smirnov's contact with Trotsky.

Vyshinsky: Did you have direct communication with Trotsky?

Smirnov: I had two addresses.

Vyshinsky: I ask you, was there any communication?

Smirnov: I had two addresses. . . .

Vyshinsky: Answer, was there any communication?

Smirnov: If having addresses is called communication. . . .

Vyshinsky: What do you call it?

Smirnov: I said that I received two addresses.

Vyshinsky: Did you maintain communication with Trotsky?

Smirnov: I had two addresses.

Vyshinsky: Did you maintain personal communication?

Smirnov: There was no personal communication.

Vyshinsky: Was there communication by mail with Trotsky?

Smirnov: There was communication by mail with Trotsky's son.

Vyshinsky: Was the letter you received through Gaven sent by Sedov or by Trotsky?

Smirnov: Gaven brought a letter from Trotsky.

Vyshinsky: That is what I am asking you. Did you have any communication with Trotsky—yes or no?

Smirnov: I say that I wrote a letter to Trotsky and received a reply from him.

Vyshinsky: Is that communication or not?

Smirnov: It is.

Vyshinsky: So there was communication?

Smirnov: There was.

Other irrefutable facts are also established. Ter-Vaganyan, Mrachkovsky, Zinoviev and Evdokimov tell about conversations which Smirnov carried on in 1931 concerning the tasks he assigned at that time for the training of terrorists.

Vyshinsky: Did you give instructions to the group?

Smirnov: No, I did not.

Vyshinsky (to Mrachkovsky): Mrachkovsky, did Smirnov give you such instructions?

Mrachkovsky: Yes. Instructions were given in the beginning of 1931 on his return from abroad.

Vyshinsky: What did he say to you?

Mrachkovsky: That it was necessary to begin the selection of people whom we knew well, that a serious task was put before us, that the people to be selected must be resolute. He said this in his apartment.

Smirnov: Was it at my apartment? Where is my apartment?

Mrachkovsky: This was in 1931 on the Pressnya.

Vyshinsky: Did he visit you on the Pressnya?

Smirnov: Not on the Pressnya itself but in that district.

Vyshinsky: Accused Zinoviev, you said that Smirnov discussed terrorism with you more than once, discussed the necessity to expedite terroristic acts?

Zinoviev: Correct.

Vyshinsky: So what Mrachkovsky says about the terrorist group is true?

Zinoviev: Yes.

Vyshinsky: Accused Smirnov, do you think that Ter-Vaganyan, Mrachkovsky and Evdokimov are telling untruths?

Smirnov: (Does not answer.)

Vyshinsky: What then do you admit?

Smirnov: I admit that I belonged to the underground Trotskyite organization, joined the *bloc,* joined the centre of this *bloc,* met Sedov in Berlin in 1931, listened to his opinion on terrorism and passed this opinion on to Moscow. I admit that I received Trotsky's instructions on terrorism from Gaven and, although not in agreement with them, I communicated them to the Zinovievites through Ter-Vaganyan.

Vyshinsky: And, while not in agreement, you remained a member of the *bloc* and worked in the *bloc?*

Smirnov: I did not resign officially from the *bloc,* but actually I did no work.

Vyshinsky: So when you communicated the instructions, you were doing no work?

Smirnov: (Does not answer.)

Vyshinsky: What do you think, when an organizer communicates instructions, is that work?

Smirnov: Of course.

Vyshinsky: You participated in the *bloc?*

Smirnov: Yes.

Vyshinsky: And you admit that the *bloc* stood on the position of terrorism?

Smirnov: Yes.

Vyshinsky: You also admit that it stood on this position in connection with instructions received from Trotsky?

Smirnov: Yes.

Vyshinsky: And it was you who received these instructions?

Smirnov: Yes.

Vyshinsky: Consequently, it was you who got the *bloc* to adopt the position of terrorism?

Smirnov: I passed on the instructions on terrorism.

Vyshinsky: If you confirm that, after the receipt of Trotsky's instructions, the position of the *bloc* was that of terrorism, then it should be said that the *bloc* took up the position of terrorism after you received the instructions from Trotsky and passed them on to the members of the *bloc?*

Smirnov: I received these instructions, communicated them to the Trotskyites and Zinovievites, and they formed the centre. While not in agreement, I did not resign from the *bloc* officially, but actually I was not a member of the *bloc.*

Vyshinsky: Ter-Vaganyan, did Smirnov leave the *bloc?*

Ter-Vaganyan: No.

Vyshinsky: Mrachkovsky, did Smirnov leave the *bloc?*

Mrachkovsky: No.

Vyshinsky: Dreitzer, did you know that Smirnov had left the *bloc?*

Dreitzer: If giving instructions to organize terrorist groups is leaving the *bloc,* then yes.

Vyshinsky: Evdokimov, did you hear of Smirnov leaving the *bloc?*

Evdokimov: No, the very opposite; he remained a member of the centre and did active work in it.

Vyshinsky: Did he share the terroristic views?

Evdokimov: Yes, he shared them.

Vyshinsky: Accused Kamenev, what do you know about Smirnov's leaving the *bloc?*

Kamenev: I confirm that Smirnov was a member of the *bloc* all the time.

Vyshinsky: Accused Smirnov, that closes the circle.

EXAMINATION OF THE ACCUSED OLBERG

The Court then proceeds to examine the accused Olberg.

The President: Accused Olberg, do you confirm your principal testimony on terroristic work?

Olberg: I confirm it fully and completely.

Vyshinsky: How long have you been connected with Trotsky-ism?

Olberg makes a detailed statement to the effect that he was a member of the German Trotskyite organization since 1927-28. His contact with Trotsky and Sedov, Trotsky's son, began in 1930. This contact was arranged by an active member of the German Trotskyite organization, Anton Grilevich, the publisher of Trotsky's pamphlets in German. At first contact was established

86

by correspondence with Sedov, who passed Trotsky's commissions on to Olberg; and in the spring of 1931, in May, when Sedov arrived in Berlin, their personal acquaintance began.

Vyshinsky: Did you meet Sedov frequently?

Olberg: From May 1931 to the end of 1932 we met nearly every week, and sometimes twice a week. We either met in a cafe on Nürnbergerplatz, or I would visit him in his apartment.

Olberg then proceeds to relate the events preceding his first visit to the Soviet Union.

Olberg: The first time Sedov spoke to me about my journey was after Trotsky's message in connection with Trotsky's being deprived of the citizenship of the U.S.S.R. In this message Trotsky developed the idea that it was necessary to assassinate Stalin. This idea was expressed in the following words: "Stalin must be removed."

Sedov showed me the typewritten text of this message and said: "Well, now you see, it cannot be expressed in a clearer way. It is a diplomatic wording." Sedov also said that it was necessary to send a number of people to the Soviet Union; it was then that Sedov proposed that I should go to the U.S.S.R. He knew that I spoke Russian and he was sure that I could gain a foothold there.

A difficulty arose about the passport. I did not have any definite citizenship, and for that reason alone could not obtain a *visa*. Soon, however, I was able to fix it up, and when I obtained a passport in the name of Freudigmann, I left for the U.S.S.R.

Before my departure for the Soviet Union, I intended to go to Copenhagen with Sedov to see Trotsky. Our trip did not materialize, but Suzanna, Sedov's wife, went there. On her return she brought a letter from Trotsky addressed to Sedov, in which Trotsky agreed to my going to the U.S.S.R. and expressed the hope that I would succeed in carrying out the mission entrusted to me. Sedov showed me this letter.

Vyshinsky: What do you know about Friedmann?

Olberg: Friedmann was a member of the Berlin Trotskyite organization, who was also sent to the Soviet Union.

Vyshinsky: Are you aware of the fact that Friedmann was connected with the German police?

Olberg: I heard about that.

Vyshinsky: Connection between the German Trotskyites and the German police—was that systematic?

Olberg: Yes, it was systematic and it was done with Trotsky's consent.

Vyshinsky: How do you know that it was done with Trotsky's knowledge and consent?

Olberg: One of these lines of connection was maintained by myself. My connection was established with the sanction of Trotsky.

Vyshinsky: Your personal connection with whom?

Olberg: With the fascist secret police.

Vyshinsky: So it can be said that you yourself admit connection with the Gestapo?

Olberg: I do not deny this. In 1933 there began organized systematic connection between the German Trotskyites and the German fascist police.

The accused Olberg then proceeds to give an account of circumstances and facts directly relating to his visits to the U.S.S.R. He went to the Soviet Union three times.

The first time Olberg went to the U.S.S.R. was at the end of March, 1933, when he travelled with a false passport in the name of a certain Freudigmann. He had obtained this passport in Berlin. Olberg remained in the Soviet Union up to the end of July 1933. The purpose of the visit was to prepare and carry out the assassination of Comrade Stalin.

On arriving in the U.S.S.R. Olberg lived secretly in Moscow for six weeks, and then went to Stalinabad, where he obtained a position as teacher of history. As he had no documents regarding military service, he was obliged to return abroad and went to Prague.

From Prague Olberg wrote to Sedov informing him about his failure.

Sedov replied saying that he must not lose heart and promised to try to obtain a better passport.

Meanwhile Olberg himself succeeded in obtaining a passport in Prague. His younger brother, Paul Olberg, lived in Prague and was connected with Tukalevsky, an agent of the German secret police in Prague. Paul Olberg cheered up his brother, stating that Tukalevsky could help him in "this trouble."

Olberg: After 1933 I visited Tukalevsky with my younger brother.

Vyshinsky: Who is Tukalevsky?

Olberg: Tukalevsky is the director of the Slavonic Library of the Ministry of Foreign Affairs in Prague. I learned from my brother that he was an agent of the fascist secret police. Tukalevsky had been informed that I would visit him, and he told me that he would try to get the necessary documents for me.

Then, continues Olberg, I wrote a letter to Sedov in Paris telling him about the proposal made by the agent of the Gestapo, and asked him to inform me whether L. D. Trotsky would approve of an arrangement with such an agent. After some time I received a reply sanctioning my actions, that is to say, my understanding with Tukalevsky. Sedov wrote saying that the strictest secrecy was necessary, and that none of the other members of the Trotskyite organization was to be informed about this understanding.

Through Tukalevsky and through a certain Benda, Olberg obtained a passport from Lucas-Parades, Consul-General of the Republic of Honduras in Berlin, who had arrived in Prague at that time.

Olberg: He sold me the passport for 13,000 Czechoslovak kronen. This money I received from Sedov.

Vyshinsky: Did you have any connection with the Republic of Honduras?

Olberg: No, never.

Vyshinsky: Permit me to show this: is this the passport? (The commandant of the Court presents the passport.)

Olberg: Yes, that is the one. It really was issued by a real consul in the name of the Republic of Honduras. There is such a republic in Central America.

Vyshinsky: Perhaps your parents had some connection with that republic?

Olberg: No.

Vyshinsky: Your forefathers?

Olberg: No.

Vyshinsky: And you yourself—where are you from?

Olberg: I am from Riga.

This time, continues Olberg, I intended to travel to the U.S.S.R. by way of Germany. Tukalevsky advised me to meet Slomovitz in Berlin. I had known her previously. Tukalevsky told me that the Berlin Trotskyites had concluded an agreement with the Gestapo and that if I met Slomovitz in Berlin I could obtain assistance and help from her if I needed it.

I visited Slomovitz in Berlin, and she told me the following: During my absence the Trotskyite cadres dwindled to a small group, and they were now confronted with the dilemma: either to dissolve or to come to an agreement with the German fascists. The basis for the agreement was the preparation and carrying out of acts of terrorism against the leaders of the C.P.S.U. and the Soviet government. Trotsky had sanctioned the agreement between the Berlin Trotskyites and the Gestapo, and the Trotskyites were in fact left free.

From the point of view of the Berlin Trotskyites, the overthrow of the Soviet system, the fight against the Soviet government, was conceivable in two ways: either by intervention, or by individual terroristic acts. The assassination of Kirov, according to Slomovitz, showed that terroristic acts against the leaders of the Party and the government could be carried out in the Soviet Union.

In Slomovitz's apartment I met an employee of the Gestapo, to whom she introduced me, and he informed me that if I needed assistance he would willingly help me in preparing terroristic acts, in the first place against Stalin.

In March, 1935, Olberg arrived in the Soviet Union for the second time. This visit was also fruitless because he had a tourist *visa,* could not stay long, and had to return to Germany after a few days. There he remained for three months, and again received instructions from Sedov to make another attempt. In July 1935 Olberg again went to the Soviet Union.

After remaining in Minsk for a short time, he went to Gorky, and there he established contact with the Trotskyites Yelin and Fedotov. He soon obtained employment in the Gorky Pedagogical Institute, where he remained until his arrest. It was here, in

Gorky that plans were worked out for an attempt on the life of Comrade Stalin.

Vyshinsky: Did you obtain the Honduras passport after your second return?

Olberg: The second time also I came on the Honduras passport.

Vyshinsky: Did you come on a tourist *visa*?

Olberg: Yes, but I had the Honduras passport.

Vyshinsky: How were you able to get an extension of that passport the second time?

Olberg: I managed that . . . I forgot to say that at this time my brother moved to the Soviet Union.

Vyshinsky: There is a gap here in your testimony. In what capacity did your brother, Paul Olberg, arrive here?

Olberg: What tasks Tukalevsky gave him I do not know. But I advised him to go to the Soviet Union so that he could help me to gain a foothold.

Vyshinsky: Why did he have to help you in gaining a foothold?

Olberg: He is an engineer, and it was much easier for him to obtain employment. He had genuine documents. At any rate, not such fictitious papers as I had.

Vyshinsky: So your brother arrived in the U.S.S.R. on a genuine German passport, and as an engineer could more easily gain a foothold here?

Olberg: Yes.

Vyshinsky: Did your brother have any connection with the Gestapo?

Olberg: He was Tukalevsky's agent.

Vyshinsky: An agent of the fascist police?

Olberg: Yes.

Vyshinsky: When did you have that talk with Sedov about not permitting the Trotskyite organization to be compromised?

Olberg: That was at the time of my second journey. He said that if I were arrested by the organs of state security of the U.S.S.R., I was under no circumstances to say that this terroristic act was carried out on Trotsky's instructions, and at all events, I was to try to conceal Trotsky's role.

91

Vyshinsky: Whom did he advise you to throw the blame on for the organization of terroristic acts?

Olberg: On the White Guards, on the Gestapo.

Vyshinsky: Consequently, we may put it this way: you, Valentine Olberg, were connected with Trotsky through his son Sedov; you were sent on Trotsky's direct instructions, conveyed through Sedov, to the U.S.S.R. as Trotsky's agent to prepare and carry out a terroristic act against Comrade Stalin?

Olberg: Yes.

Vyshinsky: In order to ensure the success of this work, you were connected through your brother with the German police?

Olberg: Yes, that is so.

Vyshinsky: Now tell us how you prepared the terroristic act.

Olberg states that even before his arrival in Gorky he learned from Sedov that an underground Trotskyite organization existed in the U.S.S.R., the leaders of which were Smirnov and Mrachkovsky. He also knew about Bakayev, whom Sedov referred to as a man with "extreme terroristic" inclinations. In Gorky Olberg learned from Fedotov that action detachments had been organized before his arrival. All that he had to do was to draw up the plan for the attempt at assassination

The terroristic act was to have been committed in Moscow on May 1, 1936.

Vyshinsky: What prevented you from carrying out this plan?

Olberg: The arrest.

Vyshinsky: Did you inform Sedov of the progress of the preparations for the terroristic act?

Olberg: Yes, I wrote him several times at Slomovitz's address. And I received a letter from her stating that our old friend insisted that the thesis for the diploma be submitted by May 1.

Vyshinsky: Thesis for the diploma—what is that?

Olberg: The assassination of Stalin.

Vyshinsky: And the old friend—who is that?

Olberg: The old friend—that is Trotsky.

EXAMINATION OF THE ACCUSED BERMAN-YURIN

The Court proceeds to examine the accused Berman-Yurin.

The President: Berman-Yurin, tell us what instructions you received abroad before your departure for the Soviet Union?

Berman-Yurin: I received instructions from Trotsky to go to the Soviet Union to commit a terroristic act against Stalin. I visited Trotsky personally in Copenhagen in November 1932. The meeting was arranged by Sedov.

In reply to Comrade Vyshinsky's questions, Berman-Yurin tells of his acquaintance of long standing with Trotsky's son, Sedov, and of his Trotskyite activities beginning with 1931. He was introduced to Sedov by one of the leaders of the German Trotskyites, Grilevich. Then Berman-Yurin goes on to speak of his meetings with Sedov.

Berman-Yurin: I had a number of talks with Sedov. Sedov systematically tried to persuade me, and convinced me, that the fight against the Communist Party was a fight against Stalin. At the end of 1931 Sedov asked me to see him and wanted to know whether I knew a trusted and reliable German who could carry out an important mission which would involve a journey to Moscow. I mentioned the name of Alfred Kundt whom I knew as a staunch Trotskyite.

On Sedov's proposal, Berman-Yurin met Alfred Kundt and communicated to him the conversation he had had with Sedov. Kundt agreed to go to Moscow. The mission was as follows: he had to take to a certain address in Moscow two documents from Trotsky, one of which was Trotsky's instructions on the tasks of the terrorist underground organization in the U.S.S.R. In Moscow Alfred Kundt was to establish personal contact with Smirnov and hand him the two documents.

Berman-Yurin: One document concerned Trotsky's latest position on questions referring to the international situation, mainly Germany. I read the second document very carefully. It was written in the handwriting of Sedov and it contained Trotsky's directions concerning the tasks of the Trotskyite underground organization in the U.S.S.R. The letter stated that it was necessary to prepare to adopt resolute and extreme means of struggle, and that with this in view, resolute people sharing Trotsky's position had to be selected. Particular attention, stated the letter, was to be paid to the Trotskyites who were members of the C.P.S.U., but who were not compromised as Trotskyites in the ranks of the

93

Party. The organization was to be built up on the principles of strictest secrecy, in small groups, not connected with each other, so that the discovery of one group might not lead to the discovery of the whole organization.

Alfred Kundt left for Moscow in January-February 1932. A few days later it became known that he had been at the secret address, had handed over the documents, had received the reply as had been arranged, but had not met Smirnov as the latter was not in Moscow. Kundt also reported that he had settled near Moscow, that he had achieved some success in his work, and that "things were going all right."

Berman-Yurin deals in detail with the circumstances of his meeting and conversation with Trotsky in Copenhagen.

Berman-Yurin: In November 1932 I had a meeting with Sedov which I remember very well because Sedov then, for the first time, spoke openly about the necessity of preparing to assassinate the leaders of the C.P.S.U. Evidently, Sedov noticed that I was wavering and he said that Trotsky would be in Copenhagen shortly and asked me whether I would not like to go there and meet Trotsky. I, of course, expressed my agreement.

I arrived in Copenhagen early in the morning. This was at the end of November, between the 25th and the 28th of November, 1932. I was met at the station by Grilevich and we went to see Trotsky. Grilevich introduced me to Trotsky and left; I remained in the room alone with Trotsky.

Now I come to my conversation with Trotsky. I had two meetings with him. First of all he began to sound me on my work in the past. He asked me why I had gone over to the position of Trotskyism. I told him about this in great detail. Then Trotsky passed to Soviet affairs. Trotsky said: The principal question is the question of Stalin. Stalin must be physically destroyed. He said that other methods of struggle were now ineffective. He said that for this purpose people were needed who would dare anything, who would agree to sacrifice themselves for this, as he expressed it, historic task.

With this the first conversation came to an end. Trotsky went somewhere. Berman-Yurin remained in the apartment and waited for his return.

94

Berman-Yurin: In the evening we continued our conversation. I asked him how individual terrorism could be reconciled with Marxism. To this Trotsky replied: problems cannot be treated in a dogmatic way. He said that a situation had arisen in the Soviet Union which Marx could not have foreseen. Trotsky also said that in addition to Stalin it was necessary to assassinate Kaganovich and Voroshilov.

Vyshinsky: What other questions did he touch upon besides questions of terrorism?

Berman-Yurin: Trotsky also expressed his views on the situation in the event of intervention against the Soviet Union. He adopted an absolutely clear defeatist attitude. He also said that the Trotskyites must join the army, but that they would not defend the Soviet Union.

Vyshinsky: Did he convince you?

Berman-Yurin: During the conversation he nervously paced up and down the room and talked of Stalin with exceptional hatred.

Vyshinsky: Did you give your consent?

Berman-Yurin: Yes.

Vyshinsky: Did your conversation end there?

Berman-Yurin: I also had a talk with Trotsky about the following. After I had given my consent he said that I must get ready to go to Moscow, and as I would have contact with the Comintern I was to prepare the terroristic act taking advantage of this contact.

Vyshinsky: So Trotsky not only gave you general instructions, but also formulated your task in a concrete way?

Berman-Yurin: He said that the terroristic act should, if possible, be timed to take place at a plenum or at the congress of the Comintern, so that the shot at Stalin would ring out in a large assembly. This would have a tremendous repercussion far beyond the borders of the Soviet Union and would give rise to a mass movement all over the world. This would be an historical political event of world significance. Trotsky said that I should not have contact with any Trotskyites in Moscow, and that I should carry on the work independently. I replied that I did not know anybody in Moscow and it was difficult for me to see how I should act under these circumstances. I said that I had an acquaintance named Fritz David, and asked whether I might not get in touch with him.

95

Trotsky replied that he would instruct Sedov to clear up this matter and that he would give him instructions to this effect.

This conversation took place at the end of November, 1932. Berman-Yurin left for Moscow in March, 1933. Before his departure Sedov instructed him to get in touch with Fritz David and to prepare the terroristic act in conjunction with him. Soon after his arrival in Moscow Berman-Yurin met Fritz David, and together they discussed the terroristic plan and began to make preparations to carry it out. At first they thought it possible to make an attempt on Comrade Stalin's life at the XIII Plenum of the E.C.C.I. Fritz David was to have secured an admission ticket for Berman-Yurin who was to shoot at Stalin. On the eve of the Plenum, however, it was found that no ticket could be obtained for Berman-Yurin. and the plan failed. It was decided to postpone the assassination of Comrade Stalin until the Congress of the Comintern.

Berman-Yurin: The Congress was to have been convened in September 1934. I gave Fritz David a Browning pistol and bullets to hide. But before the opening of the Congress Fritz David informed me that he had again failed to obtain a ticket for me, but that he himself would be at the Congress. We agreed that he should be the one to commit the terroristic act.

Several days later I met Fritz David, and he said that he could not manage to shoot. He was sitting in a box in which there were many people and there was no possibility of shooting. Thus, this plan failed too.

In December Fritz David informed me that an emissary from Sedov and Trotsky had been to see him recently and wanted to know why the terroristic act had not been committed. Fritz David gave him detailed information, and received instructions to take advantage of another opportunity, to expedite the preparations for the act and to take advantage of some conference or reception to which I or Fritz David were to gain entry at all costs and there to assassinate Stalin.

In May 1936 Fritz David informed me that another emissary —a German—had arrived from Trotsky and visited him, and had spoken to him extremely sharply, accusing us of being inactive, irresolute, lacking courage, and had literally demanded that we take advantage of any opportunity that might arise to assassinate Stalin. We must make haste, we must not lose time, he said.

At the end of May 1936 I was arrested and my terroristic activities were stopped.

At the end of the examination of Berman-Yurin Comrade Vyshinsky once again questions him about his meetings with Trotsky's son, Sedov. Berman-Yurin testifies that he had had frequent meetings with him in the period from the end of 1931 to March, 1933.

Vyshinsky: Both Trotsky and Sedov raised before you the question of terrorism and urged you to agree to commit a terroristic act?

Berman-Yurin: Quite true.

Vyshinsky: You gave your consent and were sent by Trotsky?

Berman-Yurin: By Trotsky through Sedov.

After the examination of Berman-Yurin the evening session of August 20 closes.

AUGUST 21 (MORNING SESSION)

EXAMINATION OF THE ACCUSED HOLTZMAN

The morning session of August 21 begins with the examination of the accused Holtzman.

Holtzman was one of the most active members of the Trotsky-ite counter-revolutionary organization, personally connected with the leader of the Trotskyite centre in the U.S.S.R.—I. N. Smirnov.

On Smirnov's instructions he maintained contact with the Trotskyite centre abroad.

In 1932 he personally received from L. Trotsky instructions regarding preparations for terroristic acts against the leaders of the C.P.S.U. and the Soviet government.

Holtzman testifies that he has known Smirnov since 1918. In 1926 Holtzman joined the Trotskyite organization. Later on he formally broke with the Trotskyites but continued to meet them, particularly Smirnov. After a protracted denial of his illegal Trots-kyite activities, Holtzman, in reply to point-blank questions put to him by Comrade Vyshinsky, testifies that in 1931 he "accidentally" met Smirnov in the street. Smirnov proposed to meet him at his mother's apartment. In 1932 Holtzman came to the rendezvous and told Smirnov that he was to be sent abroad on official business but that "he was refusing to do this and would go reluctantly." Smirnov advised him to go. Holtzman agreed to accept the commission and to go abroad. Smirnov asked him to visit him once again before his departure.

The cross-examination of Holtzman and Smirnov establishes the fact that Smirnov preserved particular secrecy about Holtz-man, using him for particularly secret missions.

Vyshinsky: I ask you, were you a secret member of the Trotsky-ite organization acting under the guidance of Smirnov? Do you before this proletarian Court plead guilty to this or not?

Holtzman: Yes.

The State Prosecutor further establishes that the meetings in the apartment of Smirnov's mother were not accidental and that this apartment served as the regular meeting-place for Holtzman and Smirnov. In establishing the circumstances of the meetings between Holtzman and Smirnov in the apartment of Smirnov's mother, Comrade Vyshinsky puts a number of questions to Holtzman.

Vyshinsky: So you knew that at a certain time you would find Smirnov in his mother's apartment?

Holtzman: Yes.

Vyshinsky: This was Smirnov's Trotskyite meeting place?

Holtzman: As it now appears, yes.

The accused Holtzman fails to disprove the fact that on the instructions of the Trotskyite centre he remained a covert Trotskyite within the Party.

Vyshinsky: Formally you were in the Party?

Holtzman: Yes.

Vyshinsky: At the same time you were a Trotskyite?

Holtzman: A Trotskyite.

Vyshinsky: And. . . .

Holtzman: A counter-revolutionary.

Vyshinsky: And a double-dealer?

Holtzman: Yes.

Before his departure from the U.S.S.R. Holtzman went to the meeting-place and met Smirnov there, Smirnov told Holzman that when in Berlin he was to meet Trotsky's son, Sedov. Smirnov told Holtzman that he would give him a report which he was to deliver to Sedov for Trotzky. As both Holtzman and Smirnov admit, this report was to have been handed personally to Sedov for delivery to Trotsky. Smirnov gave Holtzman a telephone number by which he was to ring up Sedov. Smirnov then gave him the password which was: "I have brought greetings from Galya." Further evidence establishes the fact that Smirnov also gave Holtzman a secret code for correspondence with Trotsky, for which purpose certain pages from the *Arabian Nights* were used

On arrival in Berlin, testifies Holtzman, he telephoned Sedov and arranged to meet him. The meeting took place near the Zoological Garden. As Holtzman and Sedov did not know each other, it was agreed that both were to carry in their hands copies of the *Berliner Tageblatt* and of the *Vorwärts*. On meeting Holtzman, Sedov proposed to go by car.

Continuing, Holtzman says: "We drove off. I don't remember the street. Sedov took me to a flat. No one was there. It was on the fourth floor. There I gave him the report and the secret code. . . . Thus I met him six or eight times in the course of four months. In November I again telephoned Sedov and we met once again. Sedov said to me: 'As you are going to the U.S.S.R., it would be a good thing if you came with me to Copenhagen where my father is.' "

Vyshinsky: That is to say?

Holtzman: That is to say, Trotsky.

Vyshinsky: Did you go?

Holtzman: I agreed, but I told him that we could not go together for reasons of secrecy. I arranged with Sedov to be in Copenhagen within two or three days, to put up at the Hotel Bristol and meet him there. I went to the hotel straight from the station and in the lounge met Sedov.

About 10 a.m. we went to Trotsky. When we arrived Trotsky first of all asked me about the feelings and the attitude of the mass of the Party members towards Stalin. I told him that I intended to leave Copenhagen that day and would leave for the U.S.S.R. within several days. Then Trotsky, walking up and down the room in a rather excited state, told me that he was preparing a letter for Smirnov, but as I was leaving that day he would not write it. I must say that throughout this conversation I was alone with Trotsky. Very often Trotsky's son Sedov came in and out of the room.

Continuing, Holtzman testifies that in the course of the conversation Trotsky said that it was "necessary to remove Stalin."

Vyshinsky: What does "remove Stalin" mean? Explain it.

Holtzman: I will speak about that. Then Trotsky said that if Stalin were removed, it would be possible for the Trotskyites to come into power and to the leadership of the C.P.S.U. He also said that the only means of removing Stalin was terrorism.

Vyshinsky: Did Trotsky say that outright?

Holtzman: Yes. He said that for this purpose it was necessary to choose cadres of responsible people fit for this task. Then he said that this was to be communicated to Smirnov, but I was not to tell anybody else about it.

Vyshinsky: Only Smirnov?

Holtzman: Yes. At that moment Sedov came in and began hurrying us to finish the conversation. With this our conversation ended, and I left.

Vyshinsky: So Trotsky plainly told you that the fundamental task now (that is, in the autumn of 1932) was to assassinate Comrade Stalin? You remember for sure?

Holtzman: Yes.

Vyshinsky: So this was Trotsky's instruction?

Holtzman: Yes. Trotsky could not put it in writing, and so I accepted it in verbal form and communicated the exact sense of it on my arrival in Moscow.

Vyshinsky: That was Trotsky's verbal instruction?

Holtzman: Yes.

Under further examination Holtzman tries to evade responsibility, declaring that he did not share Trotsky's point of view about terrorism. But the accused is immediately exposed as having remained in the underground Trotzkyite organization and having continued to meet Trotskyites after his return to the U.S.S.R.

Vyshinsky: We know that some time later Smirnov received instructions on terrorism also independently of you. I am exposing you as having received these instructions. You knew that the Trotskyites had already taken up a terroristic position and yet you continued to remain a Trotskyite?

Holtzman: Yes.

Vyshinsky: Kept up connections with the Trotskyites?

Holtzman: Yes.

Vyshinsky: Hence, you continued to be a member of the Trotskyite organization?

Holtzman: Yes.

EXAMINATION OF THE ACCUSED N. LURYE

The accused Nathan Lurye is examined.

He arrived in the U.S.S.R. from Berlin on the special mission of the Trotskyite organization for the purpose of committing terror-istic acts. All his Trotskyite activities from 1927 onwards were directed towards sapping the power of the Soviet state.

Vyshinsky: With whom did you first become intimate when you became a Trotskyite?

N. Lurye: With Moissei Lurye.

Vyshinsky: When did you become intimate with him?

N. Lurye: At the end of the summer of 1927.

Vyshinsky: When did your terroristic disposition, intentions, terroristic plans originate?

N. Lurye: The training the Trotskyite organization gave me during all those years which I spent in that organization in Ger-many in the long run reduced itself to rousing hatred towards Stalin and the leadership of the C.P.S.U. In the beginning of 1932 Moissei Lurye said to me that it was time to go to the U.S.S.R. and carry on terroristic work there. This his instruction did not come as a surprise to me. It logically followed from all the preceding work. I arrived in the U.S.S.R. in April 1932 with the instruction to establish connections with the Trotskyites I had known in Germany and to carry on terroristic work together with them.

N. Lurye began by establishing connections with the Trotsky-ites in Moscow, first of all with those whom he had known in Ger-many: Konstant and Lipschitz.

N. Lurye: I told Konstant about the terroristic instructions I had received from the Trotskyite organization through Moissei Lurye. Konstant told me it was not news to him. They, too, had terroristic instructions and had even taken practical steps to carry them out. He told me that they had a terrorist group to which Konstant and Lipschitz, and also a German engineer-architect, Franz Weitz, belonged.

Vyshinsky: Who is Franz Weitz?

N. Lurye: Franz Weitz was a member of the National-Socialist Party of Germany. He arrived in the U.S.S.R. on the instructions of Himmler who at that time was chief of the S.S. and subsequent-ly became chief of the Gestapo.

Vyshinsky: Franz Weitz was his representative?

N. Lurye: Franz Weitz arrived in the U.S.S.R. on the instruc-tions of Himmler for the purpose of committing terroristic acts.

Vyshinsky: Where did you learn this?

N. Lurye: The first one to tell me about it was Konstant, but later on Franz Weitz himself told me.

The fact that a direct agent of the German political police stood at the head of the terrorist group did not in the least disturb N. Lurye and his Trotskyite associates.

"I arrived at the conclusion," said N. Lurye, "that since the Trotskyites had adopted the method of fighting with arms this had its logic, that is to say, that if a fascist offered his services for the purposes of terrorism, those services should be made use of. I continued my connections with Franz Weitz and worked under his practical guidance."

In August 1932 Franz Weitz informed N. Lurye that there was a possibility of making an attempt on the life of the People's Commissar of Defence of the U.S.S.R., Comrade Voroshilov. The terrorist group received instructions from the fascist secret service agent to proceed to action. For a long period of time N. Lurye's group was engaged in preparing the attempt on the life of Comrade Voroshilov.

President of the Court: When you were engaged in preparing the attempt on the life of Comrade Voroshilov you for a long time watched the coming and going of Comrade Voroshilov's automobile? How long were you engaged in preparing for the attempt on the life of Comrade Voroshilov?

N. Lurye: We were engaged in it from September 1932 to the spring of 1933.

President of the Court: Judging by your testimony you frequently went to Frunze Street and to the adjacent streets, armed with revolvers?

N. Lurye: Yes.

President of the Court: All three of you were armed?

N. Lurye: Yes.

President of the Court: So that you would have committed the terroristic act had a favourable moment offered itself? Why did you not succeed in doing so?

N. Lurye: We saw Voroshilov's car going down Frunze Street. It was travelling too fast. It was hopeless firing at the fast running car. We decided that it was useless.

President of the Court: You managed to see Comrade Voroshilov's car?

N. Lurye: I saw it and so did the second member of the group, Paul Lipschitz.

President of the Court: Did you cease watching Comrade Voroshilov's car?

N. Lurye: Yes.

President of the Court: For what reasons?

N. Lurye: Because we became convinced that it was useless shooting with a revolver.

President of the Court: What did you turn your attention to after that?

N. Lurye: To the acquisition of explosives.

President of the Court: What kind of terroristic act did you intend to commit?

N. Lurye: A terroristic act with a bomb.

President of the Court: You said that you turned your attention to the acquisition of explosives for the purpose of committing a terroristic act. Against whom?

N. Lurye: Against Voroshilov.

President of the Court: In the street, or on some premises?

N. Lurye: In the street.

In July 1933 N. Lurye was sent to Chelyabinsk to work in the capacity of a surgeon (his speciality).

In Chelyabinsk N. Lurye did not cease terroristic activities and did not abandon his terroristic designs. N. Lurye testifies before the Court that knowing that Comrades Kaganovich and Orjonikidze were coming to Chelyabinsk, he tried to meet them at the works and commit a terroristic act against them. He failed to carry out his intention.

In January 1936 N. Lurye left Chelyabinsk for Leningrad on a scientific mission. Passing through Moscow, he met Moissei Lurye, who gave him instructions to make an attempt on the life of Comrade Zhdanov.

President of the Court: What instructions on terrorism did Moissei Lurye give you in 1934, 1935 and 1936?

N. Lurye: I told him that I intended to make attempts on the lives of Orjonikidze and Kaganovich, but later, in January 1936, he instructed me to shoot Zhdanov at the First of May demonstration in Leningrad.

President of the Court: You regarded Moissei Lurye as your leader since you accepted such instructions?

N. Lurye: Yes.

President of the Court: When you left for Leningrad, did you undertake to carry out M. Lurye's instructions?

N. Lurye: I knew that I would take part in the First of May demonstration, and that if it were possible I would try to carry out these instructions.

President of the Court: Did you take part in the demonstration?

N. Lurye: Yes.

President of the Court: Were you armed?

N. Lurye: Yes, with a revolver.

President of the Court: Where did you obtain the weapon this year?

N. Lurye: The weapon remained in Konstant's keeping.

President of the Court: When did you take that weapon?

N. Lurye: In March 1936.

President of the Court: What type of revolver was it?

N. Lurye: A Browning.

President of the Court: What size? Medium?

N. Lurye: Yes.

President of the Court: Did you succeed in getting into the demonstration to the Uritzky Square?

N. Lurye: Yes.

President of the Court: Why did you fail to carry out the attempt on the life of Zhdanov?

N. Lurye: We marched by, too far a way.

EXAMINATION OF THE ACCUSED M. LURYE

In reply to the President, M. Lurye declares that he fully confirms the evidence he gave at the preliminary investigation.

Vyshinsky: Accused Lurye, tell me, please, what concrete steps did you take in your terroristic activity?

M. Lurye: On leaving Berlin for Moscow on March 4, 1933, I received definite instructions. I received these instructions from Ruth Fischer and Maslov, but actually they were the instructions of Trotsky himself. I had been connected with Ruth Fischer since

1924, and in opposition work in the Zinoviev faction had been connected with her since October 1925. I had been connected with Maslov since 1927 when I returned to Berlin from Moscow. The instructions were of the following character: Trotsky is of the opinion and insists, and we, that is to say, Maslov and Ruth Fischer, are in agreement with Trotsky's instruction to the effect that it is necessary to speed up the organization of terroristic acts against the leaders of the C.P.S.U. and the Soviet government, in the first place against Stalin. I received these instructions personally in verbal form from Ruth Fischer and Maslov on March 4, 1933, as I have already said.

Vyshinsky: I am waiting for your statement on the practical steps you took in this direction.

M. Lurye: On arriving in Moscow on March 9, 1933, I communicated this verbal instruction at its destination, namely, to Zinoviev's former personal emissary in Berlin, A. V. Herzberg. I was connected with Herzberg in Zinovievite work from November 1927 until his departure for Moscow at the end of 1931. I communicated this instruction not later than the middle of April. Herzberg accepted the instruction and said that this instruction from Trotsky, Ruth Fischer and Maslov was fully in accord with identical decisions already adopted by our centre in the U.S.S.R.

In reply to questions put to him by the State Prosecutor about the practical steps the accused had taken to organize terroristic acts, M. Lurye related about his three meetings with Zinoviev. During one of these meetings which took place in Zinoviev's apartment in the beginning of August 1934, Lurye gave Zinoviev detailed information about Trotsky's instructions received through Ruth Fischer and Maslov concerning the preparation of terroristic acts, and in particular, concerning the activities of the group of his namesake, Nathan Lurye.

Vyshinsky: Tell me please, were you connected with Nathan Lurye?

M. Lurye: Yes. I was connected with Nathan Lurye approximately from April 1933 to January 2, 1936.

Vyshinsky: You knew Nathan Lurye as a member of the underground Trotskyite organization?

M. Lurye: Certainly.

Vyshinsky: You knew that at that period Nathan Lurye was engaged in preparing a number of terroristic acts?

M. Lurye: Quite true.

M. Lurye then goes on to relate how he organized the attempt on the life of Comrade Orjonikidze. This terroristic act was to have been committed while Comrade Orjonikidze was at the Chelyabinsk Tractor Works. For this purpose M. Lurye had instructed N. Lurye, who was going to the Chelyabinsk Tractor Works, to take the opportunity of a possible visit to the works by Comrade Orjonikidze to commit a terroristic act against him.

Vyshinsky: In what other measures for committing terroristic acts did you participate?

M. Lurye: I took part in preparing an attempt on the life of Zhdanov.

The accused relates in detail how on January 2, 1936, he communicated to Nathan Lurye definite instructions to organize a terroristic act against Comrade Zhdanov, and promised to give him later addresses and connect him with Zaidel's terrorist group in Leningrad.

Comrade Vyshinsky then asks M. Lurye whether he was anything to add to his evidence.

M. Lurye: I can add something to Nathan Lurye's testimony and about my important conversation with Zinoviev concerning Weitz's group. Nathan Lurye informed me concretely of the work of the terrorist group organized by Weitz. Noting my perplexity when I heard about this sort of ally, N. Lurye asked me what I thought about it. I replied that my personal attitude played no role here, that I would immediately report it in proper quarters, and said to N. Lurye: if you do not receive a reply in the negative, this will mean that you are working with the knowledge of the centre.

Vyshinsky: Whom personally did you have in mind?

M. Lurye: I had contacts with A. V. Herzberg, a person enjoying the particular confidence of Zinoviev. N. Lurye did not receive a reply in the negative from me. From the time of my conversation with him in April 1933 Nathan Lurye's group, which was organized by the fascist Franz Weitz, worked with the knowledge and indisputably with the consent of the centre, and of Zinoviev personally.

Vyshinsky: Consequently, you admit that for a considerable number of years you were a member of the underground Trotskyite organization?

M. Lurye: Yes, I fully admit it.

Vyshinsky: That organization pursued terroristic aims?

M. Lurye: I admit that I brought such instructions.

Vyshinsky: You confirm that you received instructions on terrorism from Trotsky through Ruth Fischer and Maslov and communicated them to Zinoviev?

M. Lurye: Yes.

Vyshinsky: You know that the instructions were communicated?

M. Lurye. Quite definitely.

Vyshinsky: Were you connected with Nathan Lurye's group and simultaneously with the fascist agent Franz Weitz?

M. Lurye: Yes.

Vyshinsky: Did you in conjunction with Nathan Lurye prepare a number of attempts at assassination, and did you give the instructions to prepare the attempt on the life of Comrade Stalin?

M. Lurye: I did not take part in the preparations, but I communicated instructions about the attempt.

Vyshinsky: You gave instructions to prepare attempts on the lives of Orjonikidze and Zhdanov, and you not only gave instructions, but indicated the contacts?

M. Lurye: Yes, I told Nathan Lurye that he would be given an address later.

EXAMINATION OF THE ACCUSED TER-VAGANYAN

The Court proceeds to the examination of the accused Ter-Vaganyan.

In reply to questions put to him by Comrade Vyshinsky the accused Ter-Vaganyan admits that he was one of the organizers of the Trotskyite-Zinovievite centre, and also that this centre was organized on the basis of Trotsky's instructions on terrorism.

Vyshinsky: The instructions were communicated in good time to you as one of the organizers?

Ter-Vaganyan: Yes.

Vyshinsky: You admit that you personally also took part in preparing certain terroristic acts?

Ter-Vaganyan: I did not take part in preparing terroristic acts, but I did take part in the work of the centre.

Vyshinsky: You took part in terroristic work?

Ter-Vaganyan: All the work was terroristic.

Vyshinsky: During your examination on August 14 you said: "Of the persons belonging to the united Trotskyite-Zinovievite centre, about which I spoke in detail in my testimony on July 16 this year, I. N. Smirnov, Mrachkovsky, Zinoviev and Kamenev guided the practical organization and training of the terrorist group"—do you confirm that?

Ter-Vaganyan: Yes.

Vyshinsky: And you added: "Personally I worked under the instructions of Smirnov and Kamenev"—do you confirm that?

Ter-Vaganyan: Yes.

Vyshinsky: In 1931 was Smirnov disposed towards violent methods of struggle?

Ter-Vaganyan: Yes, as were all the Trotskyites surrounding Smirnov.

Continuing his testimony, Ter-Vaganyan, speaking of his return to Moscow from Transcaucasia, confirms the testimony of the witness Safonova to the effect that she, Safonova, had informed Ter-Vaganyan about Smirnov's journey abroad and his meeting with L. Sedov.

"I must say," testifies Ter-Vaganyan, "that there was no talk at all about these instructions regarding terrorism being the personal opinion of Sedov. Had Safonova told me that this was Sedov's personal opinion, she and I would have laughed at it as a joke. When Smirnov returned, he repeated his story to me and Safonova."

Replying to Comrade Vyshinsky's question as to the reasons why Smirnov denies this, Ter-Vaganyan explains to the Court that Smirnov is afraid of telling the court the whole truth because he would then have to name a number of persons who were associated with terrorism. In particular, says Ter-Vaganyan, Smirnov does not want to say that beginning with 1928 he maintained systematic connections with Gruzian deviationists. When Smirnov returned from abroad, in 1932, he met the Gruzian deviationists, whose attitude, as is well known, was terroristic from 1928 onwards.

Vyshinsky: Smirnov, you confirm that you were connected with the Gruzian deviationists?

Smirnov: In 1929 I met Okudjava.

Vyshinsky (to Ter-Vaganyan): When did the Stückgold group exist?

Further examination of Ter-Vaganyan throws light on I. N. Smirnov's connections with the Stückgold terrorist group. Ter-Vaganyan says:

"I was introduced to Stückgold by I. N. Smirnov in 1929. Smirnov asked me receive Stückgold whenever he would arrive. He did not want Stückgold to see anyone else. Such secrecy could only have one meaning, namely that Stückgold had some kind of special connections which had to be safeguarded."

In reply to a question put to him by Comrade Vyshinsky I. N. Smirnov denies that he introduced Stückgold to Ter-Vaganyan and that he visited the latter's apartment with him. However, on being proved wrong by Ter-Vaganyan, he has to admit that such a meeting may have taken place.

Vyshinsky (to Smirnov): You admit that you may have visited Ter-Vaganyan with Stückgold?

Smirnov: I do as regards 1929.

Vyshinsky: So in 1929 you, Ter-Vaganyan and Stückgold did meet?

Smirnov: Possibly.

Ter-Vaganyan (to Smirnov): That was in the winter of 1929-30?

Smirnov: Yes.

Vyshinsky (to Ter-Vaganyan): The Stückgold group was a terrorist group?

Ter-Vaganyan: Yes, it was terrorist.

"In the autumn of 1931," continues Ter-Vaganyan, "my very close connection and friendship with Lominadze began. I met Lominadze frequently, and on these occasions we talked about a *bloc.*"

Continuing his testimony, Ter-Vaganyan says that at that period the Trotskyites began negotiations for union with the Zinovievites and the "Leftists," and that the terroristic stand was perfectly clear.

Vyshinsky: When was that?

Ter-Vaganyan: After Smirnov came back from Berlin.

Vyshinsky: At that period was the terroristic stand clear?

Ter-Vaganyan: Yes, it was clear, because the instructions had already been brought.

In clarifying the question as to the basis on which the *bloc* with the "Leftists" was formed, Comrade Vyshinsky puts a number of questions to the accused Smirnov. Smirnov's replies make it clear that the *bloc* was formed on a terroristic basis.

Vyshinsky (to Smirnov): Did you organize the *bloc* or not?

Smirnov: I instructed Ter-Vaganyan to negotiate with Lominadze.

Vyshinsky: What for?

Smirnov: For a union.

Vyshinsky: Did the union take place?

Smirnov: Yes.

Vyshinsky: With the "Leftists"?

Smirnov: Yes.

Vyshinsky: Did you join the *bloc?*

Smirnov: Yes.

Vyshinsky: At that time the instructions regarding terrorism were in operation?

Smirnov: Yes.

In reply to Comrade Vyshinsky's question as to his personal terroristic activities, Ter-Vaganyan stresses the point that he carried on terroristic work under the guidance of Smirnov and Kamenev. In particular, he discussed the question of terrorism with the Trotskyites, Zaidel and Friedland. "In 1932," says Ter-Vaganyan, "I met Friedland and told him that it was now necessary to adopt violent forms of struggle against the Party. In reply to his question as to the meaning of violent forms of struggle, I said: you are not a child—violent forms of struggle are terroristic forms of struggle. That is clear."

By a number of questions Comrade Vyshinsky clarifies the relations between Ter-Vaganyan and Friedland in terroristic activities. The replies of Ter-Vaganyan make it clear that Ter-Vaganyan gave Friedland instructions regarding the organization of terroristic acts.

AUGUST 21 (EVENING SESSION)

EXAMINATION OF THE ACCUSED FRITZ DAVID
(KRUGLYANSKY)

At the evening session of August 21, the last of the accused, Fritz David (Kruglyansky), is examined.

Fritz David was sent to the Soviet Union by Trotsky as a terrorist with instructions to make an attempt on the life of Comrade Stalin. In reply to a question put to him by the President of the Court the accused confirms his testimony as to the instructions he received personally from Trotsky in Copenhagen. In order not to expose the underground Trotskyite organization to any risk, Fritz David did not establish contact with anybody in the U.S.S.R. except with Berman-Yurin. This, declares the accused, was in pursuance of the direct instructions of Trotsky.

Replying to questions put to him by Comrade Vyshinsky, Fritz David gives to the Court a detailed account of how in August 1932 he established contact with Sedov, and, through the latter, with Trotsky.

Vyshinsky: When did you meet Trotsky?

Fritz David: I met him at the end of November 1932.

Vyshinsky: How did you come to him?

Fritz David: I travelled on a false passport. In one of the conversations I had with Sedov he told me that Trotsky was to come to Europe and would like to see me.

Vyshinsky: Tell me, during that meeting with Trotsky, was there talk of terrorism?

Fritz David: There was.

Vyshinsky: On whose initiative?

Fritz David: On Trotsky's initiative.

In his testimony regarding the content of his conversation with Trotsky, Fritz David declares that Trotsky said that the advent

112

of the Trotskyites to power in the U.S.S.R. was possible only if Stalin were physically destroyed

One of the prospects put forward by Trotsky was to take a defeatist attitude in the event of war, but he stressed the point that "there is a closer prospect of the Trotskyites coming to power— the prospect of the physical removal of Stalin."

Vyshinsky: What was your attitude toward this idea?

Fritz David: I accepted this second prospect.

Vyshinksy: Did you tell him so—that you accepted this line, that you agreed?

Fritz David: Yes.

Vyshinsky: What else occurred?

Fritz David: Then Trotsky gave me two instructions. The first instruction concerned secrecy.

Vyshinsky: You told him you would undertake a terroristic mission?

Fritz David: Yes. He proposed that I go to the U.S.S.R. and personally commit a terroristic act, without the aid of others, without any organization, without contacts with other Trotskyites.

Vyshinsky: And that is what the instruction concerning secrecy amounted to?

Fritz David: Yes. Trotsky told me that this affair involved risk and that there was no point in exposing the Trotskyite organization in the U.S.S.R. to that risk. The second instruction was to the effect that this terroristic act was to bear an international character, was to be committed at an international assembly. This shot, as Trotsky expressed it, was to reverberate throughout the whole world.

Vyshinsky: Did your conversation end at that?

Fritz David: Our conversation, which was a very long one. ended at that. Besides, Trotsky said, for example, that talk about individual terror not being compatible with Marxism was a subject for the Philistines of Marxism.

Vyshinsky: What other instructions did Trotsky give you?

Fritz David: Trotsky instructed me to behave in the U.S.S.R. in such a way as not to show any deviations from the general line of the Party, and when writing for the press to adhere strictly to the Party line, and under no circumstances to reveal the threads after the terroristic act was committed.

Fritz David arrived in the U.S.S.R. in March 1933 and met Berman-Yurin who sought him out on Sedov's instructions. Fritz David and Berman-Yurin drew up two concrete plans for attempts on the life of Comrade Stalin; the first was to be made at the Thirteenth Plenum of the E.C.C.I., the second at the Seventh Congress of the Comintern. Both plans failed, because Comrade Stalin did not attend the Thirteenth Plenum, while only Fritz David was able to get into the Congress of the Comintern, since he had failed to obtain a ticket for Berman-Yurin. Fritz David, according to his statement, was unable to commit the terroristic act because it was impossible to get near Comrade Stalin.

Vyshinsky: So you gained entry to the Congress?

Fritz David: Yes, I was at the Congress.

Vyshinsky: Why was the terroristic act not committed?

Fritz David: The indictment quite correctly states that I was not able to get near Stalin.

Vyshinsky: You went to the Congress to make an attempt at assassination?

Fritz David: Of course.

After the Seventh Congress messengers from Trotsky's son, Sedov, visited Fritz David on two occasions, and in Sedov's name accused the terrorists of not being sufficiently active and ordered them to speed up the terroristic act in accordance with Trotsky's instructions.

Vyshinsky: These meetings took place on the basis of your terroristic plans?

Fritz David: These meetings were caused by the fact that the terroristic act was not committed at the Seventh Congress, and this made Sedov furious.

Vyshinsky: But did your terroristic disposition pass away after this, or did it continue until quite recently?

Fritz David: Yes, it continued.

Vyshinsky: Until when?

Fritz David: Until my arrest.

Vyshinsky: So we may sum up. You were a member of the

Trotskyite organization and met Trotsky personally. Trotsky personally commissioned you to go to the U.S.S.R. to commit a terroristic act and warned you to observe strict secrecy. That explains why you made no contacts with any other members of the Trotskyite organization except Berman-Yurin. Together with Berman-Yurin, who had received analogous instructions, you made preparations for an attempt on the life of Comrade Stalin, timing it for the Seventh Congress in 1935. Thanks to the contacts you had in the Comintern you personally gained entry to the Congress in order to commit this act, but you failed to do so owing to circumstances over which you had no control.

Fritz David: I question this last point somewhat, not in order to minimize my guilt, but simply to present the whole picture.

Vyshinsky: Then let's say: owing to objective circumstances?

Fritz David: Owing to objective and subjective factors.

Vyshinsky: But you will not deny the charge against you that you failed to commit the act because you could not get nearer to the platform and had no chance to get near Comrade Stalin?

Fritz David: That was one of the reasons.

Vyshinsky: Yes, one of the reasons, but an obvious, objective reason. All the rest is mere psychology.

This concludes the examination of the accused Fritz David.

STATEMENT BY COMRADE VYSHINSKY, STATE ATTORNEY OF THE U.S.S.R.

After the examination of the accused at the evening session of August 21, Comrade Vyshinsky, State Attorney of the U.S.S.R. makes the following statement:

"At preceding sessions some of the accused (Kamenev, Zinoviev and Reingold) in their testimony referred to Tomsky, Bukharin, Rykov, Uglanov, Radek, Pyatakov, Serebryakov and Sokolnikov as being to a greater or lesser degree involved in the criminal counter-revolutionary activities for which the accused in the present case are being tried. I consider it necessary to inform the Court that yesterday I gave orders to institute an investigation of these statements of the accused in regard to Tomsky, Rykov, Bukharin, Uglanov, Radek and Pyatakov, and that in accordance with the results of this investigation the office of the State Attorney will institute legal proceedings in this matter. In regard to Serebryakov and Sokolnikov, the investigating authorities are already in possession of material convicting these persons of counter-revolutionary crimes, and, in view of this, criminal proceedings are being instituted against Sokolnikov and Serebryakov."

*   *   *

At the end of the evening session of August 21, the accused Dreitzer, replying to questions put to him by Comrade Vyshinsky concerning certain details of the counter-revolutionary activities of the Trotskyite-Zinovievite centre, declares that one of the active participants in the terroristic work of the Trotskyites was Putna, an old and active Trotskyite. According to Dreitzer, Putna at one time ostensibly left the Trotskyites in pursuance of the line of double-dealing, but actually continued until quite recently to carry on strictly secret work for the Trotskyite centre. In particular, Dreitzer testifies that Putna had direct contact with Trotsky, met I. N. Smirnov, and in 1932 communicated to Smirnov, through Dreitzer, Trotsky's verbal instructions to organize terrorist groups. The accused Smirnov tries to deny the fact that Putna participated in the terroristic activity of the Trotskyites. However, in reply to questions put to them by Comrade Vyshinsky, the accused Pickel, Reingold and Bakayev corroborate Dreitzer's testimony.

On the conclusion of the examination of the accused, Comrade Ulrich, President of the Court, declares the court investigation ended.

AUGUST 22 (MORNING SESSION)

The President of the Court grants leave to the State Prosecutor, Comrade A. Y. Vyshinsky, State Attorney of the U.S.S.R., to address the Court.

SPEECH FOR THE PROSECUTION

Vyshinski: Comrades judges, comrades members of the Military Collegium of the Supreme Court of the Soviet Union: For three days you have very carefully and with the greatest attention examined the evidence and proof submitted to you by the State Prosecution against the people sitting here in the dock charged with having committed the gravest crimes against the state. With the greatest possible care you have subjected to investigation and judicial scrutiny every one of these proofs, every fact, every event, every step taken by the accused, who in the course of many years added crime to crime in their struggle against the Soviet state, against the Soviet power, against our Party and against the whole of our Soviet people.

Horrible and monstrous is the chain of these crimes against our socialist fatherland; and each one of these crimes deserves the severest condemnation and severest punishment. Horrible and monstrous is the guilt of these criminals and murderers, who raised their hand against the leaders of our Party, against Comrades Stalin, Voroshilov, Zhdanov, Kaganovich, Orjonikidze, Kossior and Postyshev, against our leaders, the leaders of the Soviet state. Monstrous are the crimes perpetrated by this gang which not only made preparations to commit terroristic acts. but actually murdered one of the best sons of the working class, one of the most devoted to the cause of socialism. one of the most beloved

117

disciples of the great Stalin, the fiery tribune of the proletarian revolution, the unforgettable Sergei Mironovich Kirov.

But monstrous as these crimes are, and however profoundly we may have been stirred and digusted by this nightmare of horrible crime, you, comrades judges, as befits a Soviet court and Soviet justice, have been weighing and appraising very calmly the facts which came before you in connection with the criminal activities of these persons whose names have long ago been covered with contempt and disgrace in the eyes of the whole people.

We have now come to the end of our judicial proceedings. We are making the final summary. We are drawing our last deductions in preparation, within a few hours, perhaps, to hear your verdict, the verdict of the Court of the land of Soviets which demands and expects from you a just, unfaltering and implacably stern decision concerning the fate of these people, these contemptible murderers, these vile and insolent enemies of the land of Soviets, of the Soviet people.

We are building a new, socialist society, a new, Soviet state, under the difficult conditions of class struggle, amidst the fierce resistance of the last remnants of the exploiting classes which we have routed and utterly crushed.

Every step in our progress is accompanied by desperate resistance on the part of our enemies who rouse against us all the forces of the old world, all the filth, all the scum of the old society, who mobilize and throw into the struggle against us the most criminal, the most hardened, the most incorrigible, decayed and dishonest elements.

Lenin taught us that "there has never been a single deep and mighty popular movement in history without filthy scum,"* without the bourgeois and petty-bourgeois element fighting against the Soviet Government, and resorting not only to the methods of the Savinkovs, the Gotzes, the Gegechkoris and Kornilovs, of plots and rebellions, of floods of lies and slander, but also utilizing all the elements of decay, and embarking upon every possible sordid and shameful crime.

Comrade Stalin warned us that:

* Lenin, *Collected Works*, Vol. XXII, p. 457, Russian edition, "Immediate Tasks of the Soviet Government."

"We must bear in mind that the growth of the power of the Soviet state will increase the resistance of the last remnants of the dying classes. It is precisely because they are dying, and living their last days that they will pass from one form of attack to another, to sharper forms of attack, appealing to the backward strata of the population, and mobilizing them against the Soviet power. There is no foul lie or slander that these 'have-beens' would not use against the Soviet power and around which they would not try to mobilize the backward elements. This may give ground for the revival of the activities of the defeated groups of the old counter-revolutionary parties: the Socialist-Revolutionaries, the Mensheviks, the bourgeois nationalists in the centre and in the outlying regions; it may give grounds also for the revival of the activities of the fragments of counter-revolutionary opposition elements from among the Trotskyites and the Right deviationists. Of course, there is nothing terrible in this. But we must bear all this in mind if we want to put an end to these elements quickly and without great loss."*

Three years ago Comrade Stalin not only foretold the inevitable resistance of elements hostile to the cause of socialism, but also foretold the possibility of the revival of Trotskyite counter-revolutionary groups. This trial has fully and distinctly proved the great wisdom of this forecast.

The "heroes" of this trial have linked their fate with the fascists, with the agents of secret-police departments; these "heroes" have lost all scruples and gone to the uttermost limits of duplicity and deceit, elevated perfidy and treachery to a system, to the law of their struggle against the Soviet state.

This trial has completely revealed and has once again proved how great and boundless is the rage and hatred of our enemies toward the great cause of socialism; this trial has shown how insignificant are these enemies who rushed headlong from one crime to another. A contemptible, insignificant, impotent group of traitors and murderers thought that by means of their sordid crimes they could cause the heart of our great people to cease to beat! This contemptible, insignificant group of adventurers tried with

* Stalin, *The Results of the First Five-Year Plan*, end of Section VII.
119

their mud-stained feet to trample upon the most fragrant flowers in our socialist garden.

These mad dogs of capitalism tried to tear limb from limb the best of the best of our Soviet land. They killed one of the men of the revolution who was most dear to us, that admirable and wonderful man, bright and joyous as the smile on his lips was always bright and joyous, as our new life is bright and joyous. Thy killed our Kirov; they wounded us close to our very heart. They thought they could sow confusion and consternation in our ranks.

To the murderers' treacherous shot of December 1, 1934, the whole country replied with unanimous execration. The whole country, millions and tens of millions of people, were aroused and once again proved their solidarity, their unity, their loyalty to the great banner of the Party of Lenin-Stalin. The land of Soviets rose up like an unshakable, iron wall in defense of its leaders, its guides, for every hair of whose heads these criminal madmen will answer with their lives. In this boundless love of millions of toilers for our Party, for its Central Committee, and for our Stalin and his glorious comrades-in-arms, in this infinite love of the people lies the strength of the defence and protection of our leaders, the guides of our country and Party, against traitors, murderers and bandits.

Our great fatherland is joyously flourishing and growing. The fields of innumerable collective farms are rich with a golden harvest. Thousands of new socialist, Stakhanov factories and works are pulsating with life. Harmoniously and wonderfully our railways are working for the welfare of our fatherland, and from end to end of the country Krivonoss passenger and freight trains are speeding over the glistening ribbons of steel. Firm as granite stands our Red Army, surrounded with the love of the people, guarding the frontiers of our native land. The names of our wonderful Bolsheviks, the tireless and gifted builders of our state— Sergo Orjonikidze, Klim Voroshilov, Lazar Moisseyevich Kaganovich, the leaders of the Ukrainian Bolsheviks—Kossior and Postyshev, and the leader of the Leningrad Bolsheviks, Zhdanov, are near and dear to the hearts of us and all those who are filled with filial love for their motherland. With great and unsurpassed love, the toilers of the whole world utter the name of the great teacher and leader of the peoples of the U.S.S.R.—Joseph Vissarionovich Stalin!

Under the leadership of the Soviet government and our Party, headed by Stalin, socialism has finally and irrevocably triumphed in our country. Under the leadership of our Party the proletariat of our country took the implements and means of production from the capitalists, abolished the capitalist system which is based on private property, on exploitation, on poverty and slavery.

Under the leadership of our Party and the Soviet government the peoples of the U.S.S.R. brought about the great industrialization of our country, increased its means of production tenfold, multiplied its national wealth and thereby created the conditions for a happy and joyous life for all the toilers of the Soviet land of socialism. The victory of socialism is first and foremost the victory of our own Bolshevik Party, of its Leninist-Stalinist general line, of its Leninist-Stalinist leadership, of its Central Committee, headed by the great Stalin.

On the basis of these victories there has been created the indestructible union of all the toilers for the further reinforcement and development of socialism; there has been created and cemented the union and friendship of all the peoples of the U.S.S.R. for the building of socialism, for defence against our enemies, against the enemies of socialism. These victories have completely changed the entire face of our country, which has been raised to an unprecedented level of economic and cultural development.

These victories have brought the working class of the U.S.S.R. enormous improvement in their material well-being. It is now many years since unemployment has been eliminated and the seven-hour day, against which the "heroes" now in the dock always persistently and treacherously fought, has been introduced. Our country has achieved unprecedented successes, impossible in any capitalist country, in developing a new, really human, socialist culture.

These victories have brought our whole country, every factory worker and collective farmer, every office worker and intellectual, a happy and a well-to-do life. And these victories are the guarantee of the unity of all the Soviet people with our government, with our Party and with its Central Committee. Are not the wide, mass, popular conferences, conceivable only in our country, of the leading people of our factories and works, of our transport system, of our cotton and sugar beet fields, of live-stock breeders, of combine and tractor drivers, of Stakhanovites and Krivonossites with the leaders of the Party and the government the best proof of this indestructible, genuine unity and solidarity of the masses of the people with the great Stalin, with our Central Committee, with our Soviet government? This is a manifestation of genuine Soviet, true democracy! And is not the mighty wave of popular wrath, now sweeping from one end of the country to the other against these despicable murderers, a striking evidence of this unity?

The Trotskyite-Zinovievite Centre—A Gang of Contemptible Terrorists

During the preceding days of the trial these gentlemen tried to strike a "noble" attitude. They, or at all events their leaders, spoke about their terroristic plot with a certain pose; they sought and expected a political evaluation of their crimes, they talked about political struggle, about some kind of political agreements with some kind of alleged political parties. And although they admitted that in reality they had no political platform, that they did not even feel the need to draw up a political platform because, on their own admission, their platform could be written at one sitting, in a couple of hours, nevertheless, they tried to pose as genuine political figures. They do all they can to make it appear that they are standing on some political position, bespattered and battered, perhaps, but political none the less. These efforts are merely a false screen to conceal their political emptiness and lack of principle. And when they spoke about the interests of the working class, about the interests of the people, when they will speak about this, in their speeches in their defence and in their last pleas, they will lie as they have lied hitherto, as they are lying now, for they fought against the only people's policy, against the policy of our country, against our Soviet policy. Liars and clowns, insignificant pigmies, little dogs snarling at an elephant, this is what this gang represents!

But they know how to use guns, and therein lies the danger to society. This makes it necessary to adopt special and most severe measures against them. To chain them is not enough. We must adopt more determined and radical measures against them. Not political figures, but a gang of murderers and criminals, thieves who tried to rob the state, this is what this gang represents!

These gentlemen admitted that they had no program; but they did have some sort of a "program." They had a program both in home and foreign policy. In their home policy their program could be put in one word—to murder. It is true that they prefer to speak not of murder but of terror. But we must call things by their proper names. These gentlemen chose murder as a means of fighting for power. They were compelled to admit this here themselves, cynically and openly.

How did these gentlemen reconcile their alleged Marxism with the preaching of terror and terroristic activity? In no wise! And yet these people called themselves Marxists at one time! Probably the accused Zinoviev still considers himself a Marxist. He said here that Marxism could not be reconciled with terrorism; but Marxism can explain how they came to terrorism.

During this trial I asked the accused Reingold how they reconciled Marxism with the preaching of terror and terroristic activities, and he said: "In 1932, Zinoviev, in Kamenev's apartment, in the presence of a number of members of the united Trotskyite-Zinovievite centre, argued in favour of resorting to terror as follows: although terror is incompatible with Marxism, at the present moment these considerations must be abandoned. There are no other methods available of fighting the leaders of the Party and the government at the present time. Stalin combines in himself all the strength and firmness of the Party leadership. Therefore Stalin must be put out of the way in the first place." Here you have a reply, frankly cynical, insolent, but absolutely logical. Here you have the sum and substance of Zinoviev's new "philosophy of the epoch."

Reingold said: "Kamenev enlarged on this theory and said that the former methods of fighting, namely, attempts to win the masses, combinations with the leaders of the Rightists, and banking on economic difficulties, have failed. That is why the only method of struggle available is terrorism, terroristic acts against Stalin and his

123

closest comrades-in-arms, Voroshilov, Kaganovich, Orjonikidze, Kossior, Postyshev and Zhdanov."

This is frank and insolent, but at the same time it is logical from the point of view of the logic of the class struggle, from the point of view of the logic of our enemy who is fighting against the land of socialism.

Without the masses, against the masses, but for power, power at all costs, thirst for personal power—this is the whole ideology of the gang that is now in the dock.

The whole cynical unprincipledness of these people was frankly avowed here by Kamenev. In his explanations before the court he stated how and on what basis this terroristic conspiracy, as he called it, was organized.

Kamenev said: "I became convinced that the policy of the Party, the policy of its leadership, had been victorious in the only sense in which the political victory in the land of socialism is possible, that this policy was recognized by the masses of the toilers."

This statement is remarkable for its lack of principle and for its insolent cynicism: just because "the policy of the Party had been victorious," they fought against its leaders.

Kamenev said: "Our banking on the possibility of a split in the Party also proved groundless. Two paths remained: either honestly and completely to put a stop to the struggle against the Party, or to continue this struggle, but without any hope of obtaining any mass support whatsoever, without a political platform, without a banner, that is to say, by means of individual terror. We chose the second path."

The accused Kamenev should have been more consistent: if he called the first path the path of honest renunciation of the struggle, then he should have called the second path the path of dishonest struggle with dishonest weapons.

He admitted: "We chose this second path. In this we were guided by our boundless hatred of the leaders of the Party and the country, and by a thirst for power, with which we were once closely associated and from which we were cast aside by the course of historical development."

The accused Zinoviev said: "At the end of 1932 it became evident that our hopes had proved false...the fact was that the general line of the Party was winning." "Here," said Zinoviev, "the complete lack of principle and ideals which brought us to the bare and unprincipled struggle for power became strikingly apparent." (Vol. XII, p. 34.)

After this, can we speak with these people in any sort of political language? Have we not the right to say that we can speak with these people in one language only, the language of the Criminal Code, and regard them as common criminals, as incorrigible and hardened murderers.

Such was their "program" in the sphere of home policy, if one may so express it. Formerly, if only out of shame, they gave as grounds for their struggle against the leaders of the Soviet government and the Party, shortcomings, defects and difficulties. Now they have already thrown off this mask. Now they admit that they had become convinced that socialism in our country was victorious. They came to terrorism, to murder, because their position had become hopeless, because they realized that they were isolated from power, from the working class. They came to terrorism because of the complete absence of favourable prospects for them in the fight for power by other methods and by other means.

Kamenev admitted that the organization of terror was the only means by which they hoped to come to power and that it was precisely on this basis of terroristic struggle that negotiations which finally resulted in the union of the Trotskyites and Zinovievites were conducted and successfully concluded. Terrorism was the real basis on which the Trotskyites and Zinovievites united.

Not all of them want to admit that.

Comrades judges, in drawing up your verdict in your council chamber, you will carefully—I have no doubt about that—once again go over not only the material of the court investigation but also the records of the preliminary investigation and you will become convinced of the animal fear with which the accused tried to avoid admitting that terrorism was precisely the basis of their criminal activities.

That is why Smirnov wriggled so much here. He admits that he was a member of the centre, he admits that this centre had adopted a terroristic line of struggle, he admits that he himself received from Trotsky the instructions about this terroristic struggle. But at the same time he tries by every means in his power to prove that he, Smirnov personally, did not adopt terror, did not agree with it, and he even went so far as to say that he had left the Trotskyite-Zinovievite terrorist centre or *bloc.*

I will come back to each one of the accused, including Smirnov, and try as fully, carefully and objectively as possible to analyze the evidence which proves that they committed the gravest crimes against the state. At present I merely wish to emphasize once again that the accused are not political infants, that they are hardened players in the political struggle; they know perfectly well that they must answer not only for recognizing terror "theoretically" —for this alone they should have paid with their heads—but for having translated this "theoretical" program into the language of terroristic practice, into the language of practical, criminal activity.

Trotsky, Zinoviev, Kamenev—Sworn Enemies of the Soviet Union

Terror was the basis of all their activities, it was the basis of the Trotskyite-Zinovievite union. This was quite unanimously testified to by people who were not directly connected with each other in their underground work. This was not only admitted here by Zinoviev and Kamenev, Smirnov and Ter-Vaganyan, Reingold and Pickel; it was stated also by Berman-Yurin, Fritz David and Valentine Olberg, that peculiar citizen of the Republic of Honduras, paid agent of Trotsky and simultaneously of the German secret police—the Gestapo.

All these persons, under the weight of evidence against them, could no longer deny and had to admit that the main, in fact the only means of struggle against the Soviet government and the Party which united their criminal activity was terror, murder.

Reingold said: "The Trotskyites and all the members of the *bloc* insisted and agreed on this." It was precisely the removal through violence of the leaders of the C.P.S.U. and the Soviet government that was the fundamental aim of this Trotskyite-Zinovievite *bloc,* which can be quite fairly called, as I called it in the indictment, an association of political assassins.

126

These terroristic sentiments which formed the basis of the organization of the Trotskyite-Zinovievite *bloc* in 1932-36 were perhaps most distinctly and characteristically expressed by the accused Mrachkovsky, who stated both at the preliminary investigation and at this trial:

"Hopes for the collapse of the policy of the Party must be regarded as doomed. The methods of struggle applied up to now have not produced positive results. Only one path of struggle remained, and that was the path of removing by violence the leaders of the Party and the Government."

Mrachkovsky said: "The principal task is to put Stalin and the other leaders of the Party and the Government out of the way."

All their bestial rage and hatred were directed against the leaders of our Party, against the Political Bureau of the Central Committee, against Comrade Stalin, against his glorious comrades-in-arms.

It was upon them, headed by Comrade Stalin, that the main burden of the struggle against the Zinovievite-Trotskyite underground organization lay. It was under their leadership, under the leadership of Comrade Stalin, that great executor and keeper of Lenin's will and testament, that the counter-revolutionary Trotskyite organization was routed. It was under their leadership, amidst fierce battles against Trotskyite counter-revolution that Trotskyite counter-revolution was finally crushed.

In the fighting against this Trotskyite counter-revolution, Comrade Stalin developed and undeviatingly carried out Lenin's teachings on the building of socialism in our country, having armed the vast millions of workers and collective farmers with these teachings.

That is why the Trotskyites and Zinovievites, as well as the other most frenzied counter-revolutionary elements, concentrated all their efforts and their hatred and rage against socialism on the leaders of our Party. That is why in March 1932, in a fit of counter-revolutionary fury, Trotsky burst out in an open letter with an appeal to "put Stalin out of the way" (this letter was found between the double walls of Holtzman's suit case and figured as an exhibit in this case).

Trotsky addressed this despicable appeal with still greater

frankness to a number of his disciples abroad whom he had recruited as assassins to be sent to the U.S.S.R. for the purpose of organizing terroristic acts and attempts on the lives of the leaders of our Soviet state and our Party. This was related in detail here by the accused Fritz David. He stated that in November 1932 he had a conversation with Trotsky during which Trotsky said literally the following: "Now there is no other way out except the removal by violence of Stalin and his adherents. Terror against Stalin—that is the revolutionary task. Whoever is a revolutionary—his hand will not tremble." (Vol. VIII, p. 62.) For this purpose Trotsky recruited high-strung persons, impressing upon them that they must commit this counter-revolutionary act as if it were some sort of "historic mission."

Berman-Yurin testified here that Trotsky systematically and repeatedly said: "Until Stalin is removed by violence, there will be no possibility of changing the policy of the Party; in the fight against Stalin we must not hesitate to adopt extreme measures— Stalin must be physically destroyed."

Fritz David and Berman-Yurin discussed with Trotsky the assassination of Stalin. They accepted Trotsky's commission and took a number of practical steps to carry it out. Does not this in itself deserve the sternest punishment provided for by our law—— death by shooting?

Fritz David, Berman-Yurin, Reingold, V. Olberg, and I. N. Smirnov himself have in fact utterly exposed Trotsky's role in this matter. Even Smirnov, who stubbornly denied that he took any part in the terroristic activities of the Trotskyite-Zinovievite centre, could not help admitting that he personally had received the directions on individual terror against the leaders of the Soviet government and the C.P.S.U. in 1931 from Trotsky's son, Sedov, that these directions on terror were confirmed by Trotsky in 1932 in the instructions brought from abroad by Gaven and conveyed to Smirnov. Smirnov tried to alleviate the gravity of his own position by stating that the instruction on terror which he had received from Sedov was Sedov's personal attitude. But this is a worthless explanation. It is obvious to everyone that Sedov was no authority whatever for Smirnov. Ter-Vaganyan and Mrachkovsky corroborated this here when they said that had they thought that the direction on terror came from Sedov they would have spat upon it with supreme contempt.

The accused Ter-Vaganyan, one of the principal organizers of the united centre, confirmed that Smirnov, while abroad, really did receive from Trotsky instructions to adopt terror. Ter-Vaganyan merely veiled his evidence by substituting for the word terror the phrase: "sharp struggle against the leaders of the C.P.S.U." Later, however, he had to decipher this and to admit that these were instructions, the content of which was terrorism and terrorism alone.

Finally, you heard the witness Safonova whose confrontation with the accused has probably left a deep impression upon the memories of everyone present in this court. At this confrontation, Safonova, whose case is being taken up separately because the investigation is still continuing, fully confirmed that Smirnov received from Trotsky instructions on individual terror through Sedov in 1931, and later through Gaven.

On the basis of these facts we can take it as absolutely established that it was precisely Trotsky's instructions on terrorism that served as the basis for the development of the terroristic activities of the united centre. Trotsky's instructions to organize a united centre and to adopt terrorism were accepted by the Trotskyite underground organization. Zinoviev and Kamenev, the leaders of the Zinovievite section of the *bloc,* arrived at the same idea and also accepted Trotsky's instructions as the basis of the activities of the united centre and underground organizations.

These bitter and ingrained enemies could not look calmly on the growing prosperity of our people, of our country, which had emerged onto the highroad of socialism.

The U.S.S.R. is achieving victory. The U.S.S.R. is building socialism, in the U.S.S.R. socialism is triumphant, and because of that their hatred towards the Central Committee, towards Stalin and the government to whom the country owes this victory, of whom the country is proud, grows more and more.

From their gloomy underworld Trotsky, Zinoviev and Kamenev issue the despicable call: Put out of the way, kill! The underground machinery begins to work, knives are sharpened, revolvers are loaded, bombs are charged, false documents are written and fabricated, secret connections are established with the German political police, people are sent to their posts, they engage in revolver practice, and finally they shoot and kill.

That is the main thing! The counter-revolutionaries not only dream of terror, they not only devise plans for a terroristic plot, or for terroristic attempts, they not only prepare to commit these foul crimes, they commit them, they shoot and kill!

The main thing in this trial is that they transformed their counter-revolutionary thoughts into counter-revolutionary deeds, their counter-revolutionary theory into counter-revolutionary terroristic practice; they not only talk about shooting, they shoot, shoot and kill!

That is the main thing. They killed Comrade Kirov, they were getting ready to kill Comrades Stalin, Voroshilov, Kaganovich, Orjonikidze, Zhdanov, Kossior and Postyshev. This is what we are trying these people for, these organizers of secret murder, these certified murderers.

And that is why we demand that the Court judge them as severely as our Soviet law commands, judge them as our socialist conscience demands.

Murder—this is the whole "program" of the home policy of these people.

What was their foreign policy?

Here the shades of the dead arise, here the old "Clemenceau theses" are revived, here the cloven hoof of Trotsky again becomes visible.

Trotsky's letter received by Dreitzer contained three brief points: 1) put Stalin and Voroshilov out of the way; 2) unfold work of organizing nuclei in the army; 3) in the event of war, take advantage of every setback and possible confusion to seize the leadership.

This is avowed banking on defeat.

This is the old Clemenceau thesis, but in a new version, edited by the united centre of the Trotskyite-Zinovievite terroristic *bloc*.

Fritz David stated during the preliminary investigation and confirmed it in this Court (and it fully conforms with a number of historical documents, the evidence of other accused and the very nature of the task which confronted Trotsky, Zinoviev and Kamenev), that in one of his conversations with Trotsky the latter asked him: "Do you think this discontent will disappear in the event of a war between the Soviet Union and the Japanese?" (He referred to the discontent which he thought existed in our country.) "No, on the contrary," said Trotsky, "under these conditions the forces hostile to the regime will try to unite, and in that case our task will be to unite and take the lead of these discontented masses, to arm them and lead them against the ruling bureaucrats" (Vol. VIII, p. 61).

Trotsky repeated this in his letter of 1932 (evidently this is his *idée fixe*) and in a conversation with Berman-Yurin.

Berman-Yurin stated: "In connection with the international situation at that time Trotsky told me that the task of demoralizing our military forces was of particular importance, for in the event of a war against the Soviet Union large masses would be called up to the army." Trotsky and the Trotskyites together with the Zinovievites calculated on being able to influence these masses very easily. "Trotsky said to me literally the following," added Berman-Yurin: " 'We will defend the Soviet Union provided the Stalin leadership is overthrown' " (Vol. IV, p. 100).

Such was their program in foreign policy!

Perhaps this is all an invention? Perhaps Fritz David and Berman-Yurin just gave rein to their fantasy? Perhaps this is all a pack of lies, an invention, the irresponsible chatter of the accused who are trying to say as much as they can against the others in order to mitigate their own ultimate fate? No! This is not an invention, not fantasy! It is the truth! Who does not know that Trotsky, together with the accused Kamenev and Zinoviev now in the dock, several years ago proclaimed the "Clemenceau thesis," that they said that it was necessary, in the event of war, to wait until the enemy had got within a distance of 80 kilometers of Moscow and then to rise in arms against the Soviet government, to overthrow it. This is an historical fact. It cannot be denied. And that is why it must be admitted that the evidence given by Berman-Yurin and Fritz David in this connection corresponds to the truth.

Such was the "foreign policy" program of these people. For this program alone our Soviet people will hang these traitors on the very first gates! And it will serve them right!

Double-dealing, Deception and Provocation—The Principal Methods of the Trotskyites-Zinovievites

Let us now turn to the methods by which these people operated. This, perhaps, is one of the most shameful pages in the story of their shameful criminal activities.

In conformity with the "principle" of the Trotskyite-Zinovievite underground *bloc* to seize power by any means, the members of this *bloc* widely practised double-dealing as their principal method in their relations with the Party and the Government. They transformed this double-dealing into a system which all the Azefs and Malinovskys, all the secret police, with all their spies, provocateurs and agents for diversive activities, might well envy.

Reingold stated that in 1933-34 Zinoviev told him in a private conversation—and Zinoviev corroborated this before the whole world at this trial—that "the principal, practical task that confronted their underground organization was to organize their terroristic work so secretly as not to compromise themselves in any way."

Perhaps this is an exaggeration? Of course not. What Reingold said conforms to the logic of things.

"The main thing during an investigation," said Zinoviev in instructing his accomplices, "is to deny all connection with the organization, arguing that terror is incompatible with the views of Bolsheviks-Marxists" (Vol. XXVII, p. 112).

Trotsky also recommended that in the event of a terroristic act being committed, they should dissociate themselves from the Trotskyite organization and take up a position analogous to that taken by the Central Committee of the Socialist-Revolutionaries toward Madam Kaplan who shot at Vladimir Ilyich (Lenin). We know what that means. We remember that after Kaplan fired her treacherous bullet at Lenin, the Central Committee of the Socialist-Revolutionaries issued a leaflet in which they categorically declared that they had nothing to do with this terroristic act. Trotsky, Zinoviev and Kamenev adopted the same tactics.

Zinoviev said: "We took the path of a carefully considered and profoundly secret plot, we regarded ourselves as Marxists, and remembering the formula 'insurrection is an art,' altered it to suit

132

our purposes and declared that 'plotting against the Party, against Stalin, is an art.' "

The masters of this "art" are now sitting in the dock. I will not say that they are highly skilled masters. They are unskilled masters. Nevertheless, they managed to do their despicable work. What did their "art" consist of? The foremost part of their plan was by every possible means to mask their truly criminal faces.

This perhaps is one of the most striking cases in history when the word mask acquired its real meaning: these people put masks on their faces, adopted the pose of repentant sinners who had broken with the past, who had abandoned their old erring ways and mistakes which grew into crime.

It is characteristic that precisely at the time when the united Trotskyite-Zinovievite centre was intensifying its activities to the utmost, when these terroristic activities reached their highest point of development, when they were advancing to the consummation of the despicable murder of Comrade Kirov, it was precisely at that period that Zinoviev sent a letter of repentance to the Central Committee. In this letter dated May 8, 1933, that is to say, when the preparations for terroristic acts were at their height, Zinoviev not only renounced all his past mistakes, but hypocritically vowed his loyalty to socialism and to the Party.

During the very days in which he was preparing to strike a treacherous blow at the very heart of the Party, preparing a terror- istic act against Comrade Stalin, this criminal who, like all those sitting in the dock at the present time, had lost every semblance of a human being, ended his letter with the following words:

"I ask you to believe that I am speaking the truth and nothing but the truth. I ask you to restore me to the ranks of the Party and to give me an opportunity of working for the common cause. I give my word as a revolutionary that I will be the most devoted member of the Party, and will do all I possibly can at least to some extent to atone for my guilt before the Party and its Central Committee."

We know now what these words were worth, we know that Zinoviev did all he possibly could to damage the Party and the work of building socialism in our country, to damage the cause of the whole international Communist movement.

On June 16, 1933, he published an article in *Pravda* entitled "Two Parties." He publishes an article in the Central Organ of our Party in which he does everything to prove his loyalty to the Party, roundly condemns opportunism and sings hallelujahs to the victories achieved by the Party.

This was on May 8 and June 16, that is to say, in the summer of 1933. And in that very summer of 1933, as has now been definitely established, at a conference of the Trotskyite-Zinovievite centre, Zinoviev instructs Bakayev to start the practical realization of measures of terrorism.

Zinoviev was indignant with Smirnov here when the latter reproached him for telling lies. Smirnov himself did not utter a single word of truth here, but he reproached Zinoviev for telling lies. Zinoviev was offended and said that the difference between him and Smirnov was that he, Zinoviev, "had firmly decided at this last moment to speak the whole truth, whereas Smirnov had evidently taken a different decision."

Permit me, comrades judges, to warn you against this statement of Zinoviev's. Do not believe that he is really speaking the whole truth here.

At the Leningrad trial on January 15-16 Zinoviev and Kamenev performed not at all badly in one of the scenes of their cunning, perifidious masquerade. While giving evidence at the trial on January 15-16, 1935, Kamenev wanted to create the impression that he was an enemy who had finally and sincerely laid down his arms and was telling all that was in his heart against the government and the Party. He then recalled some episode in which Zinoviev concealed something of what was said in a conversation with Trotsky. In a voice of pathos and "unfeigned" indignation Kamenev reproached Zinoviev for having concealed this fact, for not speaking the truth.

But at that very time Kamenev himself, and Zinoviev, tried to deceive us, to deceive the Court and the whole country by stating that they had had no connection whatever with the murder of Sergei Mironovich Kirov. Then, as now, literally in the same words that were uttered yesterday, Zinoviev and Kamenev vowed that they were speaking the whole truth. It may be said that for Kamenev and Zinoviev the trial of January 15-16, 1935, was a sort of

134

rehearsal of the present trial, which they did not expect, perhaps, but which they did not escape any more than they could escape from fate.

I will come back to the "remarkable" evidence given at the trial in Leningrad. I mention it now only in order to warn you, and through you, through the Court, to warn the whole country, not only against Kamenev and Zinoviev, but against all other double-dealers, all other traitors whom unfortunately we still have in our ranks and who talk about their repentance, who dissociate themselves, and mask themselves, in order the better to thrust their knife into the back of the Party, of our country, of our great cause.

Not the slightest confidence must be placed in these certified and hardened deceivers!

They themselves understand that they do not deserve any confidence. While examining Zinoviev I asked him: "Are you speaking the whole truth now?" And he answered: "Now I am speaking the whole truth to the very end."

But what proof is there of this? How can we believe them when they have surpassed all conceptions of perfidy, cunning, deceit and treachery?

Zinoviev carried this perfidy to such lengths that after the murder of Sergei Mironovich Kirov he sent an obituary notice to *Pravda*. The only thing he said here about that was: "That obituary was not published as far as I remember." And that is all.

Here is the obituary; I have it in my hand. Zinoviev dated it, if I am not mistaken, the 4th or 7th of December, most probably the 4th of December.

You, Zinoviev, gave this obituary notice on Comrade Kirov the title "The Beacon Man." How did you start the obituary notice which you intended for the press, and which, consequently, was to become public property?

"This could be observed throughout the 17 years of our revolution, at every moment when the enemy contrived to strike a blow at the Bolsheviks. . . . That is what happened when the enemy succeeded in striking a palpable blow on the battlefields of the Civil War, that is what happened . . ." etc., etc.

And further on Zinoviev writes: "The grief of the Party is the grief of the whole people, of all the peoples of the U.S.S.R.

135

The Party's mourning is the mourning of the whole of our great country. . . . The whole people have felt the bitterness of bereavement."

It is true that the bitterness of bereavement and anger against the treacherous shot was felt by the whole country. That feeling was really shared by the whole country, young and old.

But to what extent does this concern you?

"The foul murder of Sergei Mironovich Kirov has in truth roused the whole Party, the whole of the Soviet Union." "The loss of this beloved and dear man has been felt by all as the loss of one who is nearest and dearest of all. . . ."

This is what you, the accused Zinoviev, wrote in this terrible and disgraceful article. Why did the Party lose this near and infinitely dear S. M. Kirov, accused Zinoviev? The Party lost this man who was so near and dear to us because you, the accused Zinoviev, killed him, you killed him with your own hands, your hands are stained with Kirov's blood! . . .

"Beloved son of the Party," you wrote. What insolent sacrilege!

"A son of the working class—this is what this Beacon Man was," "our dear, deep, strong. . . . One could not help believing him, one could not help loving him, one could not help being proud of him."

This is what Zinoviev wrote, exceeding all bounds of cynicism!

Such is this man. He loved him, he was proud of him, and he killed him! The miscreant, the murderer, mourns over his victim! Has anything like it ever occurred before?

What can one say, what words can one use fully to describe the utter baseness and loathesomeness of this: Sacrilege! Perfidy! Duplicity! Cunning!

It was you, Zinoviev, you who with your sacrilegious hand extinguished this beacon, and you began publicly and hypocritically to tear your hair in order to deceive the people.

Whom did you kill? You killed a magnificent Bolshevik, a passionate tribune, a man who was dangerous to you, a man who fought devotedly for Lenin's testament and against you.

You killed this man in a flash of time by the bullet fired by the despicable hand of Nikolayev, and two or three days after wards you sent an article to the *Pravda* in which you wrote about the "extinguished beacon." Where shall we find the word with which to appraise this despicable trick! I can not find the words in my vocabulary!

We will now pass to Kamenev, the second pillar of the so-called Zinovievite group, this hypocrite "in an ass's skin," as he himself expressed it at the Seventeenth Congress of the Party.

I ask the Court to pay attention to the articles Kamenev published in 1933. Kamenev wrote these articles almost simultaneously with those written by Zinoviev by mutual agreement. Kamenev published an article in *Pravda* in which he, like Zinoviev, renounced his past erring ways, condemned his own mistakes and said that "the man who had fought Lenin for decades became the most important figure in the opposition," etc., etc. "It is clear," wrote Kamenev in this article of May 25, 1933, "that the resistance to the policy headed by Comrade Stalin was based on the premises which made members of the Party in October 1917 come out as the opponents of the policy of Lenin." Weeping and groaning, Kamenev tried to prove that he had broken off relations with his old friends and concluded his article with an appeal to all of them to abandon all resistance which was interfering with the work of building socialism.

This was in May 1933. And in the summer of 1933, after the return of Kamenev and Zinoviev from exile, a meeting of the Trotskyite-Zinovievite centre was held in Zinoviev's apartment for the purpose of organizing terroristic acts against the leaders of the Party and the Soviet government.

When Kamenev was asked about this here, his replies were curt. The following dialogue took place between me and him, which I will take the liberty to repeat. I asked:

"What appraisal should be given the articles and statements you wrote in 1933, in which you expressed loyalty to the Party? Deception?

"*Kamenev:* 'No, worse than deception.'

"*Vyshinsky:* 'Perfidy?'

"Kamenev: 'Worse!'

"Vyshinsky: 'Worse than deception; worse than perfidy—find the word. Treason?

"Kamenev: 'You have found the word!' "

Later on he said that he not only did this in agreement with Zinoviev, but that it was all done in fulfilment of the plan to seize power that had been drawn up beforehand, which plan was combined with the necessity of winning confidence.

There is a small detail which is of some importance for defining the moral, or, if you will, the ideological level of the accused Kamenev, for characterizing his interests at the time, for characterizing some of his moral premises.

I would like to mention one of the books of Machiavelli (Vol. I). It was published in 1934 by the "Academia" Publishing House, of which Kamenev was then the head, and has a preface by Kamenev. It is a very interesting book. It was written in the 16th century. The author wrote it for a prince in order to instruct him in the art of governing the state in accordance with his princely interests. Machiavelli wrote: "You must know that there are two ways of contending, by law and by force: the first is proper to men; the second to beasts.

"But because many times the first is insufficient, recourse must be had to the second. A prince must possess the nature of both beast and man."

This pleased Kamenev very much, and in his short preface to this book he wrote the following interesting words: "A master of political aphorism and a brilliant dialectician...." (According to Kamenev Machiavelli was a dialectician! This hardened schemer turns out to be a dialectician!) "A master of political aphorism. . . ." A fine aphorism indeed! Machiavelli wrote: to fight by means of laws is characteristic of men, to fight by means of force is characteristic of the beast; pursue this bestial policy and you, says Machiavelli, will achieve your goal. And this the accused Kamenev calls being a "master of political aphorism."

Let us hear what Kamenev writes further: ". . . A dialectician who from his observations had formed the firm opinion that all concepts of the criteria of good and evil, of the per-

138

missible and impermissible, of the lawful and criminal were relative. . . ." Evidently, according to Kamenev, this is dialectics: mixing up what is criminal with what is not criminal, the lawful with the unlawful, good with evil is a new "Marxian" interpretation of dialectics à la Machiavelli.

"Machiavelli," wrote Kamenev in 1934, "made his treatise into an astonishingly sharp and expressive catalogue of the rules by which the ruler of his time was to be guided in order to win power, to hold it and victoriously to withstand any attacks upon it." You had a good teacher, Kamenev, but you, and you must be given credit for this, have excelled your teacher.

Further on you write in this preface: "This is far from being the sociology of power, but from this prescription there magnificently stand out the zoological features of the struggle for power in the society of slave owners based on the rule of the rich minority over the toiling majority."

That is so. But you wanted to employ in our society the methods of struggle and the principles of struggle that were worthy of slave owners; you wanted to apply them against our society, against socialism. You write: "Thus, this secretary of the Florentine bankers and their ambassador at the Pope's Court, by accident or design, created a shell of tremendous explosive force which disturbed the minds of rulers for centuries. . . ." You, Kamenev, adopted the rules of Machiavelli, you developed them to the utmost point of unscrupulousness and immorality, you modernized them and perfected them.

I do not ask you, comrades judges, to regard this book as material evidence in this case. I am not using this book to prove that the accused are guilty of the crimes of which they are charged. I simply thought it necessary to devote a few minutes of attention to this circumstance, in order to show the ideological source from which Kamenev and Zinoviev obtained their sustenance at that time—these men who even now, at this trial, try to preserve their noble pose of Marxists capable of thinking and arguing in conformity with the principles of Marxism.

Drop this clownish farce! Tear the mask from your faces

once and for all! Here Kamenev calls Machiavelli's book a shell of enormous explosive force. Evidently Kamenev and Zinoviev wanted to use this shell to blow up our socialist fatherland. They miscalculated! And although Machiavelli was a puppy and a yokel compared with them, nevertheless, he was their spiritual preceptor. "Machiavellism," and Azefism served you as the source of your activities and your crimes. Now this has been exposed by Zinoviev and Kamenev themselves: murder, cunning, perfidy and masquerade were the principal, decisive methods in their criminal activities.

Yesterday, Zinoviev and Kamenev, frankly if cynically, admitted that this entered into the plan of their activities. This was testified to by Reingold, this was testified to by others of the accused, and I think that a sufficiently exhaustive characterization of these methods is contained in the materials which I have presented. Summing up this part of my speech, I can say that the Trotskyite-Zinovievite centre was organized on a terrorist basis and had its program, a very primitive and simple one, it is true, expressed in only a few words, a program which did not even need for drafting the two hours to which the accused themselves contemptuously referred. Their program of home policy was confined to murder; their program of foreign policy was confined to the defeat of the U.S.S.R. in war; their method was perfidy, cunning and treason.

The Counter-Revolutionary Terroristic Activities of the Trotskyites-Zinovievites are Fully Proved

I now pass to the second part of my speech for the prosecution, to the practical activities of the so-called united centre and to the characterization of the role of each of the accused in this criminal conspiracy against the Soviet government.

There is not the slightest doubt that the union of the Zinovievite and Trotskyite counter-revolutionary groups which took place in the autumn of 1932 arose and grew strong on the soil and on the basis of the mutual recognition of terror as the sole and decisive method in the struggle for power—a struggle which was then the fundamental and principal task of the Trotskyites and Zinovievites.

140

An organization existed. An underground, conter-revolutionary, terrorist group existed. Existed and functioned. However much Smirnov may try to deny this here, he will not succeed. The facts are too strong, the facts are too numerous. We, the prosecution, have every ground for asserting that an underground, counter-revolutionary, Trotskyite Zinovievite group existed, that this terrorist organization was created, that it was created precisely as a terrorist organization, that it developed its activities precisely as terroristic activities, that it prepared for terroristic attempts at assassination and that, to our great misfortune and horror, one of these attempts was successful. The foul murder of Sergei Mironovich Kirov on December 1, 1934, was committed by this organization. This is the most horrible of the crimes which this organization succeeded in committing.

In January 1935 we tried the Moscow centre in connection with the trial of the Leningrad centre which took place a little before that, about two weeks before, and as a result of which L. Nikolayev, Kotolynov, Rumyantsev, Sossitsky and a number of others were convicted and shot. At that time we did not yet know who were the real authors, instigators and participants in this monstrous crime. But we were on the right track. The investigation directed by the People's Commissariat for Internal Affairs proceeded along the true and correct trail of exposing the real organizers of this crime, although the amount of evidence available at that time did not enable us to make a direct charge against Kamenev, Zinoviev, Evdokimov and Bakayev of organizing this murder, of guiding this murder, of committing this murder.

The verdict in the case of the so-called Moscow centre in which Kamenev, Zinoviev, Evdokimov and several others played the principal roles merely said in regard to the role they played that they had fanned the terrorist sentiments of their accomplices, that they had created the objective soil upon which this crime inevitably had to grow up and did grow up.

Being absolutely objective, the investigating and prosecuting authorities did not then charge Kamenev, Zinoviev, Evdokimov and Bakayev with directly instigating, directly organizing this murder. The indictment stated that the investigating authorities had not established their direct participation. Nevertheless, all the materials in the possession of the investigating authorities permitted them to say that these people—Kamenev, Zinoviev, Bakayev and Evdokimov—were closely connected with this crime and, as they themselves expressed it, had to bear complete moral and political responsibility for it.

In conformity with this Kamenev, Zinoviev, Evdokimov and Bakayev were given in the Moscow centre case a relatively mild sentence—only deprivation of liberty.

Kamenev, Zinoviev, Evdokimov and Bakayev did all they possibly could to misrepresent the real state of affairs, to shield the real organizers and accomplices in the crime. They tried to make it appear that they had had no hand in this sordid and despicable affair. Speaking in lofty style, they declared that the counter-revolution had chosen them as the instrument of its criminal activity. It was not they who had chosen counter-revolution as the instrument of their struggle, it was counter-revolution which had chosen them as its instrument....

Zinoviev, Kamenev, Bakayev and Evdokimov did all they could to assert and prove that they could not bear more responsibility for this foul murder than moral and political responsibility; but they declared that they were fully and honestly prepared to bear this responsibility, and admitted the correctness and the justness of the charges brought against them within those limits.

During the trial on January 15-16, 1935, Zinoviev said: "There are many of us sitting in the dock, more than fifteen persons, each with a different biography. Among us there are many who have belonged to the working class movement for many years. Much of what they have done they did because they had confidence in me, and for that, of course, I must torture myself. The task that I see confronting me at this stage is to repent fully, frankly and sincerely, before the court of the working class, of what I understood to be a mistake and a crime, and to say it in such a way that it should all end, once and for all, with this group."

I have already said that this statement of Zinoviev's was a pose, a manœuvre, a tactical move.

This is the way criminals always behave. Accused of murder and robbery, they plead guilty only to robbery. Accused of robbery, they plead guilty only to larceny. Accused of larceny, they plead guilty only to receiving stolen goods. These are the usual tricks of criminals: charged with graver crimes, they plead guilty to lesser crimes. It is a trick to wipe out the traces of the crime committed, counting on the credulity of people who still, in many cases, even in criminal cases, show some confidence in criminals.

This was the position taken up by Zinoviev. An analogous position was taken up—and this they will not deny—by Kamenev, Evdokimov and Bakayev. Caught in 1935, almost red-handed, these people admitted responsibility for the minor crime in order to evade responsibility, real responsibility, for the major crime.

Zinoviev talked about making a "frank and sincere" confession, but he did not really do that. Actually, they did all they could to shield their accomplices from the hand of Soviet justice, to leave themselves some reserves, in order at the necessary moment to use these reserves against our Party, against the leaders of our country.

This explains the whole position taken up by Zinoviev, Kamenev, Evdokimov and Bakayev at the Leningrad trial on January 15-16, 1935. "It is true," said Zinoviev, "that we are being tried on objective features." He said that he did not know many of the people who were with him in the dock at that time. Zinoviev, it would appear, did not know either Evdokimov, or Gertik, or Kamenev, or Sakhov.... Zinoviev said that subjectively they were "loyal" to the working class.

Zinoviev even had the effrontery to allege that he and his 15 accomplices were subjectively loyal to the working class and did not want to take the path of counter-revolution, but objectively things turned out the other way. Why did things turn out the other way? I would like the accused Zinoviev in his speech in defence to say how it happened that although he was subjectively loyal to the working class, objectively it turned out the other way. This cannot be the case; such things do not happen. If, objectively, it really turned out that way, it was only because your subjective loyalty to the revolution, accused Zinoviev, was false and rotten! What were you thinking about when you said these things? I ask you to tell us about that too, in your speech in defence.

143

In your fight against the Soviet government you armed yourself not only with rage but with firearms. You carried out your criminal designs in practice. You yourself spoke about duplicity, but you spoke about it in such a way as to conceal the fact that even at that moment you were continuing the policy of duplicity.

You said: "I am accustomed to feel that I am a leader; for me, personally, that played an enormous role." You said:

"I am accustomed to feel that I am a leader, and it goes without saying that I should have known everything. If I am removed from the leadership, it is either an injustice, or a misunderstanding, or for a few months. This is no justification, but I am telling you all I think, and thereby I am extracting from my body the last splinter of the crimes that are being unfolded here."

Zinoviev extracted the "last splinter" at the Leningrad trial. . . . No! He did not do that! He left that splinter, and not only that one, but several, in the body of our socialist country in order to continue to prepare for and commit the gravest crimes.

You said:

". . . I did not think otherwise: how can I be without my circle, without knowing everything, without being in the very heart of politics," etc.?

That was the thought that was torturing you—you thought that nothing could happen without you. . . . Your position in the past was determined by deeds, just as your present position is determined by your deeds. Approaching the question as to whether there was a centre, you said: Of course there was one up to 1929. You tried to assert that there was no centre in the subsequent years, that strictly speaking it did not function after 1929. That was deception. The old Zinovievite centre was transformed into the centre of the united Trotskyite-Zinovievite *bloc*. It was reorganized, it became somewhat stronger because several groups were consolidated. In 1932 it began to develop its activities on a wider scale. In 1933 it displayed particular activity, it prepared for a number of terroristic acts, and in 1934 it committed one of them.

Zinoviev said, "this is not the centre that existed in 1926-27," and that he had no connection whatever with this centre. How did Zinoviev then put the question of connection with the Leningrad

144

centre? He said that "there was a group consisting of Kotolynov, Mandelstamm, Myasnikov and others." An important role was played by Kotolynov, which, Zinoviev alleges, he learned from the indictment in the case of Kirov's murder.

Zinoviev wanted to assert that he learned about one of the organizers of the Leningrad terrorist group only from the indictment!

Was that really the case? No, it was not. Zinoviev sent Bakayev to Leningrad to establish contacts with the Nikolayev-Kotolynov group and to investigate how Nikolayev, Kotolynov, Mandelstamm and others were preparing to commit the crime.

Here again we have deceit, lies, again camouflage!

"We sought rapprochement with them." Already in 1935, in spite of all the camouflage, Zinoviev had to admit that he had sought rapprochement with Kotolynov and Nikolayev, and that he found this rapprochement. Now this has been established with absolute precision.

Zinoviev related that in 1932 he met Levin, who was shot in 1935 in connection with the murder of Comrade Kirov, and added: "We did not talk about organization. Nor was there any need for this: my hints were understood, I was an authority for him and he was an authority for me; I knew that this man of the 'leaderless group' would do what we told him." This, too, contains a number of half hints and half admissions, which only subsequently, after a number of clues exposing Zinoviev had been collected, made it possible to ensure Zinoviev's full confession of his part in this crime. Now Zinoviev no longer conceals the fact which yesterday Bakayev tried very hard to minimize.

Already in January 1935, in connection with the Moscow centre case, Zinoviev admitted that Vladimir Levin was particularly intimate with Bakayev. But yesterday Bakayev tried to minimize this intimacy, to minimize it by stating that he did not go to meet Levin in Leningrad for conspirative, terroristic purposes. But these were the only purposes possible, where such an intimacy existed. All the time he tried to impress: expunge the words "for this purpose" from the evidence and the indictment. No, Bakayev, we shall not expunge those words; they cannot be expunged because

145

you went there "for this purpose," as an expert, an expert in terrorism, and your journey was not accidental!

Why did not Zinoviev send Reingold, Pickel or even Evdokimov to Leningrad? Why did Zinoviev choose Bakayev and no other to negotiate with the Leningrad group, with the group that was to murder Comrade Kirov? I find the reply to that question in Zinoviev's evidence, and partly in that of Bakayev, at the trial on January 15-16, 1935. Zinoviev's choice fell on Bakayev because Bakayev was most closely connected with Levin, who was the representative of the Zinovievites in Leningrad, who was the leader of the Leningrad terrorist underground organization, as he himself admitted before the Military Collegium, last year. We also find confirmation of this in Zinoviev's evidence: "Bakayev knew him particularly closely, he was one of the important organizers of the anti-Party struggle in Leningrad. . . ."

Accused Zinoviev, was it only anti-Party struggle? It was an anti-Soviet struggle, a counter-revolutionary struggle, a struggle which by its very nature bore an openly counter-revolutionary, anti-state, anti-Soviet character!

Zinoviev went on to say: "I did not give him any instructions." Well, you know this is jesuitry that can hardly be exceeded. It is like the reply of the Jesuit monk who, when asked: "Did this man pass here?" answered, pointing up his sleeve: "He did not pass here". . . .

You had no contacts with Levin, but you did have contacts with him through Bakayev. Bakayev travelled on your instructions. Consequently, when you said: "I did not give him any instructions," you lied again!

Bakayev was not the only one to carry out your instructions. All of you—both Kamenev and Zinoviev, as well as the whole of your centre, carried on negotiations with Levin, Kotolynov, Nikolayev, Rumyantsev, Sossitsky, Mandelstamm and a number of other members of this gang of Leningrad Zinovievites, which has now been broken up and destroyed. The whole of your centre checked up on the progress being made by the Leningrad gang of Zinovievites in preparing for this crime; and you waited impatiently for the time when at last that loyal son of our Party, the leader of the Leningrad Bolsheviks and fiery tribune, Sergei Mironovich

146

Kirov, would be destroyed. And they lived to see this murder committed.

In this Court Zinoviev admitted that he was pressing to hasten murder. He was in a hurry, he clutched feverishly at people like Nikolayev and Kotolynov in order to hasten this murder. Not the least motive was the desire to forestall the Trotskyite terrorists. The Trotskyites were pressing hard.

Zinoviev admitted that Smirnov was also hurrying. They were all hurrying. The Trotskyites operated with greater determination and energy than the Zinovievites. Zinoviev knew that Trotskyite terrorists were arriving from abroad. And Zinoviev declared that it was a "matter of honour"—I am ashamed to use such a word in this connection—to carry out his criminal design sooner than the Trotskyites! Hence Zinoviev's feverish impatience. That is why he was waiting every day for the moment when that treacherous shot would at last be fired in Leningrad. All .his activities were directed towards committing this foul crime as soon, as swiftly and as successfully as possible!

Such was the role played by Zinoviev, such was his conduct in this affair.

In finishing with this episode, I would like now to get a straight answer from Zinoviev to the following question: Does Zinoviev now accept only moral responsibility, or the whole criminal responsibility, full responsibility, for preparing, organizing and committing the murder of Sergei Mironovich Kirov?

Of course, Zinoviev will say "yes." He cannot say anything else. He said this on the very first day of this trial when caught in the grip of the iron chain of evidence and proof.

At that same trial Kamenev took an almost similar stand. Bakayev took a similar stand. Kamenev said that he did not know of the existence of the Moscow centre. Trying to pose as a noble person, he said that in so far as the centre existed, and this was proved, he was responsible for it. . . .

The way Kamenev put it, it amounted to this: he did not know there was a centre, but if there was a centre, well then, he knew about it. But Kamenev did know of the existence of the centre; he indeed knew. This has been proved. And now this is corroborated by fresh evidence obtained in connection with the discovery of a number of new criminal gangs operating in the same direction. This evidence throws full light on this ghastly and terrible affair.

And then Kamenev tried to pose as a man who had become politically blind. He said: I became blind—I lived to the age of 50 and did not see this centre in which, it turns out, I myself was active, in which I participated by action and by inaction, by speech and by silence.

It sounds like some sort of spiritualism, spiritualism and black magic!

Even at that time we realized that this was simply an attempt at concealment by means of false phrases, an attempt by means of these false phrases to conceal the truth. Now all this has been finally exposed. No, Kamenev did not become blind. Kamenev very well saw and knew what he was doing. He saw perfectly well what was going on around him, because he organized what was going on around him. Kamenev did not become blind, because he acted by speech and silence. By silence when he did not say: "Don't do that," when he should have said that; and by speech when he said: "Do it," when, perhaps, some of his younger assistants wavered and turned to him as their authority, as their mentor.

Kamenev said:

"I want to say—not in my own justification, I did not remember this before but now I recall—that some time ago Zinoviev told me that Safarov had visited him and had proposed some sort of a *bloc*. I said that I would not take part in any *bloc* because I never believed that man. Zinoviev can confirm this. I was not opposed to talking. I talked."

With whom did he talk?

"With Tolmazov and Shatsky." Tolmazov and Shatsky were active members of the Leningrad Zinovievite gang which killed Comrade Kirov.

Kamenev talked with Tolmazov and Shatsky, that is to say, with two of the principal organizers of the murder of Comrade Kirov. So Kamenev agreed to these conversations and carried them on through Bakayev. But he tried to conceal this.

Arguing that he could not have any connection with terrorism, Kamenev, striking a pose, said:

148

"I must say that I am not a coward by nature, but I never banked on fighting with arms. I always expected that a situation would arise in which the Central Committee would be compelled to negotiate with us, that it would move up and make room for us. . . . These dreams did not recur during the past two years, simply because I am not a dreamer and not a fantast. There were fantasts and adventurers in our midst, but I do not belong to that category."

I think that Kamenev will now define his part in this affair somewhat differently. What aim did Kamenev set himself? Did he or did he not bank on fighting with arms?

At that time he said—"No." Now, two days ago, he said—"Yes." At that time he said "no" because he knew, he saw that we were as yet not in possession of all the threads of this ghastly crime, because at that stage of the investigation all the threads had not yet been finally unravelled. At that time he said: "No." Now when everything has been disclosed, he says—"yes."

Here is a characteristic fact! It shows what a great and decisive role personal motives played in this criminal "work" of Kamenev. Kamenev thought that a time must arrive when the Central Committee would move up and make room for him. But suppose it did not move up? Suppose it did not make room for him? In that case he, Kamenev, would take measures to have room made for him.

This is the whole of Kamenev's logic and politics! Logic and politics which make it utterly impossible for us to agree that he does not belong to the category of people whom he himself described as adventurers. No. Obviously he belongs to this category, as well as to the other category—the "fantasts." There was not a little of fantasy here, but there was plenty of willingness to put this fantasy into practice, to make it real, to make it a living thing even by means of adventures, by means of a *bloc* with spies, agents for diversive activities, secret police agents, murderers, and by direct murders. Kamenev agreed to this, Kamenev was prepared to do this.

Here is something else he said at the Leningrad trial: "I am speaking before the portraits of these great builders of socialism. . . ." It must be said that among these there was a portrait framed in black, the portrait of Comrade Kirov. Kamenev at the

149

trial vowed before the portrait of Kirov, whom Kamenev had murdered!

". . . Before the portraits of these great builders of socialism I am a criminal if I lacked the strength to leave and to take with me those whom it was possible to take. . . ."

Lies! Again hypocrisy, cunning, perfidy and cynicism!

The Trotskyite-Zinovievite Centre Killed Comrade Kirov

Above I asked: Was there an organization? Was there a Trotskyite-Zinovievite terrorist centre? I answer: Yes, there was. It arose in 1932. It consisted of Kamenev, Zinoviev, Evdokimov, Bakayev, Smirnov, Ter-Vaganyan and Mrachkovsky.

This centre existed, and, what is most important, it was formed on the direct instructions of Trotsky, Zinoviev and Kamenev. It was formed on the direct instructions of Trotsky to adopt terror as the sole method of fighting against the leaders of the land of Soviets. It was formed on the basis of profound and strict secrecy. Yesterday we were able to observe one of the representatives of this Trotsky-Zinoviev-Kamenev school of conspiracy in the person of the accused Holtzman. In the dock we have another conspirator in the person of Smirnov. The centre existed and functioned: it not only resorted to methods of downright perfidy, deceit and treachery but, as has now been definitely established, it organized and established secret communications with the German fascists, with whom it mated the German Trotskyites, using them in the fight against our leaders, using their connections with the German Gestapo in the persons of Tukalevsky, P. Olberg and their like.

I take it as absolutely proven by the personal evidence of literally all the accused, including that of Smirnov on this point, that this centre was organized on a terroristic basis, that the centre resorted to terroristic methods, not shrinking from the most sordid and cynical methods in its struggle. I take it as absolutely proven that this centre prepared a number of terroristic attempts in the Ukraine, in Moscow and in Leningrad. Finally, this centre prepared and committed the murder of Sergei Mironovich Kirov in Leningrad.

As I have already said, the murder of Sergei Mironovich Kirov

was part of the conspirators' general plan to murder the leaders of
the Soviet state and the C.P.S.U. Incidentally, this has been established by the evidence of Evdokimov. I ask the Court to take note
of Evdokimov's testimony of August 10, when he said that the
murder of Kirov was committed on the direct instructions of the
united centre of the Trotskyite-Zinovievite *bloc,* when he said
that in 1934 Zinoviev gave him direct instructions to this effect.
Bakayev also corroborated this. The decision to organize the murder of Kirov was adopted by Zinoviev, Kamenev, Evdokimov and
Bakayev, and by Trotsky's representatives, Mrachkovsky and Ter-
Vaganyan.

Evdokimov's evidence, to which I now refer, reads as follows:
"For the purpose of preparing for the murder, Bakayev was sent
to Leningrad at the beginning of November 1934, that is to say,
some days before Nikolayev killed Kirov in the Smolny, in the city
of Leningrad—to check up on the preparations for this murder.
Bakayev personally met Nikolayev and on returning to Moscow informed Evdokimov, Zinoviev and Kamenev of this. The latter
noted with satisfaction the successful progress of the preparations
for this foul crime and began to wait for the shot. Bakayev warned
Nikolayev and his accomplices that they must wait for Zinoviev's
signal, that they must fire simultaneously with the shots to be
fired in Moscow and Kiev."

All this has now been proved by the trial. Let the accused
challenge this in their defence speeches if they dare.

After prolonged denials during the preliminary investigation
Zinoviev gave the evidence which I have already mentioned. A
characteristic detail. As far back as the autumn of 1932, in Zinoviev's and Kamenev's summer villa (they jointly occupied a
summer villa which, incidentally, Kamenev once called the source
of his misfortunes) Bakayev was instructed to prepare a terroristic act against Comrade Stalin, and Karev was instructed to prepare one against Comrade Kirov. But then the situation changed,
for Karev was arrested and Kamenev and Zinoviev found themselves in exile.

Then came 1933, the year of revival of terroristic sentiments,
the year of resumption of activities by the Trotskyite-Zinovievite
centre. And now, Bakayev is given instructions; and thorough

preparations for the murder of Comrade Kirov are begun.

Kamenev says: "I did not know these preparations proceeded in practice because it was not I, but Zinoviev who exercised practical direction in the organization of this terroristic act." Accused Kamenev, did you know that Bakayev went to Leningrad to check up on the progress of these preparations? Yes, you knew. Did you know that Bakayev, after having checked up and found that everything was going on successfully, arrived in Moscow and reported to you the progress of these preparations? You knew How, after this, can you presume to say that you took no practical part in the murder of Kirov? Your attempt to throw all the blame on Zinoviev will not hold water.

Kamenev says "it was decided" to kill, and adds "I agreed to this decision." Is this not taking practical steps?

At the preliminary investigation Bakayev persistently denied that he had played any part in the preparations for the murder of Kirov; but he was exposed by Karev, who reminded him of a number of facts. And only then, after that, did Bakayev confess. That is why, in view of Bakayev's full confession, I refrained from examining Karev in Court.

It was the hand of Nikolayev, of Kotolynov, of his group that murdered Sergei Mironovich Kirov. But who else took part in this murder? I asked Zinoviev: When was the united centre organized? Zinoviev replied: In the summer of 1932. During what period of time did it function? Zinoviev: Practically up to 1934. . . .

I would like to deal with this question in greater detail. In 1932-33 Kamenev and Zinoviev were in exile; but the centre functioned. It is known that in 1934 Smirnov, too, was not at liberty; he was arrested in January 1933; but the centre functioned. And Zinoviev confirms that the centre functioned. I draw the conclusion that if the centre functioned it was because of the well-organized technique of communication which enabled even those who were not at liberty, Smirnov, for example, to take part in guiding the work of this centre.

I know that in his defence Smirnov will argue that he had left the centre. Smirnov will say: "I did not do anything, I was in prison." A naive assertion! Smirnov was in prison from January 1, 1933, but we know that while in prison Smirnov organized contacts with his Trotskyites, for a code was discovered by means of which Smirnov, while in prison, communicated with his companions outside. This proves that communication existed and Smirnov cannot deny this.

But even this does not settle the question because, after all, what is important for us is that Smirnov, like Zinoviev and Kamenev, is responsible for all the centre's activities and for the activities of the whole of the terrorist group which was organized, built up and functioned under his leadership when they were still at liberty. Smirnov, Zinoviev and Kamenev were the organizers of the centre; they directed the activities of their terrorists, of all these Pickels, the Dreitzers and the rest. And they must bear full responsibility for this, irrespective of whether any one of them was at liberty at the time or not. This is elementary, and I do not think it is necessary to deal with it in detail. As the leaders, they must answer for the whole of the criminal activities of the organization which they led and of all those groups which sprang up on the soil they plowed.

What did the activities of the centre consist of? Zinoviev said: "Their principal activities consisted in the preparations of terroristic acts against the leaders of the Party and the Government." I asked: against whom? Zinoviev answered: against the leaders. I asked: that is to say, against Stalin, Voroshilov and Kaganovich? Was it your centre that organized the murder of Kirov? Was the murder of Sergei Mironovich Kirov organized by your centre, or by some other organization?

Zinoviev: Yes, by our centre.

I asked: Did this centre comprise you, Kamenev, Smirnov, Mrachkovsky and Ter-Vaganyan?

Zinoviev: Yes.

To my question: So you organized the murder of Kirov?

Zinoviev replied: Yes.

And so it is Zinoviev, Kamenev, Smirnov, Mrachkovsky, Ter-Vaganyan and all the rest who must answer for this crime.

The most persistent in his denials is Smirnov. He pleaded guilty only to being the leader of the Trotskyite underground counter-revolutionary centre. True, he said this in a somewhat jocular way. Turning to Ter-Vaganyan, Mrachkovsky and Dreitzer, he said to them: "You want a leader? Well, take me." But you, accused Smirnov, were the leader. Smirnov was the leader of the Trotskyite underground organization. It was no accident that Zinoviev and Kamenev regarded him as Trotsky's representative, as Trotsky's deputy, as the actual leader of the whole of the Trotskyite underground organization. And finally he himself confessed to this.

I do not know what Smirnov is going to say in his last plea; but I think that on the basis of the material of the preliminary investigation and of the material of the court investigation I have every ground for declaring the following: 1) the accused Smirnov has confessed that for a number of years he was the actual leader of the Trotskyite underground organization; 2) he has confessed that he was Trotsky's representative and deputy in the U.S.S.R.; 3) he has confessed that he was in Berlin in 1931 and there met Sedov; and 4) he has confessed that Sedov informed him of the terroristic tasks and gave the terroristic directions.

It is true that Smirnov denies that these were Trotsky's directions. He says that this was Sedov's "personal opinion." Nevertheless, on returning to the U.S.S.R., he considered it necessary to communicate Sedov's "personal opinion" to his companions in the underground organization. . . .

We asked him: Where is the logic of this? If this was Sedov's personal opinion, and moreover, an opinion with which Smirnov, as he asserted, did not agree, why communicate it to the other members of the underground organization? Communicate it and not say that he did not agree with it? All his companions in the counter-revolutionary underground organization declare that he did not even hint at his disagreement with this line. Under these circumstances, what can we regard as established? Was there a meeting with Sedov in 1931? There was. Is Sedov—the son of L. Trotsky—his closest and first assistant in all his political activities? He is. During this meeting, did Sedov talk to Smirnov? He did. Smirnov admits this. Did they talk about terror? Yes, they talked about terror. Smirnov admits this too. The question as to how Smirnov understood Sedov is after all a matter of complete indifference

154

to the prosecution. If Smirnov understood his conversation with Sedov not as an instruction, then there was no need for him to communicate it to his colleagues in his underground group. If he communicated this conversation and did not say that he disagreed with it, it means that it was an instruction, and it could not be otherwise.

Smirnov says that he did not agree with this instruction. But if he did not agree with it he, as a sufficiently experienced underground worker, factionalist and counter-revolutionary, should have understood that it was his duty to break with this group, to leave this group. Otherwise he would not be a man engaged in politics, let alone a leader of an underground organization. Yet Smirnov was not merely a rank-and-file member of the Trotskyite group. Smirnov is not Holtzman. Holtzman is a poor edition of Smirnov; but Smirnov is not Holtzman. Smirnov is Smirnov. He is the leader. How can the leader remain a member of an underground group when he disagrees with the main line of this group? And the main line of this group was terrorism. And if he says that in 1931 he did not accept what Sedov said as an instruction, but took it merely as Sedov's personal opinion, in 1932, however, he received direct instructions from Trotsky through Yuri Gaven. At that time he could no longer say that this was somebody's "personal opinion," for even if it really was a "personal" position, it was the position of Trotsky!

From Sedov's personal position a straight path leads to Trotsky's position. There are no personal positions! There is the Trotskyite decision, Trotsky's line of terrorism. You, Smirnov, received it in 1931 and in 1932. You also received the instruction from Dreitzer, not personally, but I am deeply convinced that you knew about it notwithstanding the fact that you were in a house of detention for political offenders.

In 1932 you received Trotsky's instruction through Gaven. Trotsky plainly said: Terror; put Stalin out of the way; kill Voroshilov; kill the leaders of the Party and the government. You, Smirnov, received this instruction. You say: I received it, but did not accept it. If you did not accept it, and if you preserved a sense of political honesty to any degree, after having heard in 1932 Trotsky's instruction sent to you through Gaven,

155

you could not but break with the Trotskyite organization. You understand this, and that is why you say—I broke, I left. But whom did you tell that you had left? You told no one. Mrachkovsky did not know about it, Ter-Vaganyan did not know about it and even Safonova did not know about it. You did not tell anyone! No one knew!

Consequently, we have no right whatever to believe these assertions of yours. We can assert that in 1932 you received instructions on terrorism from Trotsky and you accepted them. You would not be the Smirnov you are if you remained in the Trotskyite group while disagreeing with the fundamental line of this group, while disagreeing with the line of the man who was such an authority for you as was Trotsky. We know that in your defence speech you will curse Trotsky. But no one will believe you, because in this Court you have not said, and you do not want to say, even two words of truth about your work in the terrorist centre. Even yesterday you wanted to conceal the role played by Putna. You wanted to save some reserves, who, perhaps, would not be entirely exposed. You wanted to save reserves for Trotsky, for your accursed Trotskyite underground organization!

I think that all the circumstances I have mentioned permit us to establish the following in regard to Smirnov.

First. Smirnov was a member of the united centre of the Trotskyite-Zinovievite terrorist organization. This centre was organized with his participation. Consequently, he is one of the most important organizers of the centre.

Second. He organized this centre on the basis of Trotsky's instructions which he received in 1931. He gave this centre its terroristic character and the terroristic direction of its activities.

Third. In 1932, Smirnov received a second instruction from Trotsky. This is indisputably established. All Smirnov's attempts to prove that, having received this instruction, he did not agree with it, although he remained in the ranks of the Trotskyite underground organization, are too transparent.

Comrades judges, there is one other very important circumstance. The question can be put in this way: All right, terroristic basis, disposition towards terrorism, talk about terror being the

156

sole means—but what about the organization of practical measures for the purpose of getting together terrorist groups, for
the purpose of putting terrorism into practice?

Ter-Vaganyan said that work was carried on to get together terrorist groups, but that this was preparatory work
which did not go beyond the limits of preparations. But was that
really the case?

Of course not. The Zinovievites followed the Trotskyites,
and Smirnov in particular, who persuasively and fervently insisted on the earliest application of terror, and not terror in
general, but terror against Comrades Stalin, Kirov, Voroshilov,
and other of our leaders. It was Comrade Stalin and Comrade
Kirov who had smashed this dishonest opposition. It is quite
understandable, therefore, that Smirnov, this consistent, fully
convinced and irreconcilable Trotskyite, should concentrate all
his organizing abilities on preparing the assassination first of all
of the leaders of the Central Committee of our Party, the leaders of our country. Smirnov kept urging Zinoviev: Let us hurry
up and commit a terroristic act, let us hurry up and kill Stalin,
Kirov and Voroshilov. And Zinoviev, hurrying at the heels of the
Trotskyites is full of excitement and agitation fearing lest he
lag behind. . . .

Smirnov urged Zinoviev to hurry up with the murder. He
was in no hurry about a platform. He said: It could be drawn
up at one sitting. What did they want a platform for when they
had what in their opinion was a surer means—assassination!
Smirnov drew up and placed in the hands of his agents a concrete plan for the organization of terroristic acts. The murder of
Comrade Kirov was carried out in fulfilment of this plan, for
which Zinoviev as well as Kamenev, Smirnov, Mrachkovsky and
Ter-Vaganyan must bear full responsibility before the land
of Soviets, before the Soviet people, before the Soviet proletarian Court.

The Masks Are Torn From the Accused

I consider that the guilt of Zinoviev, Kamenev, Evdokimov
and Bakayev has been fully established, and that I can be re-

157

lieved of the duty of enumerating the many facts, and of analysing the material of the Court investigation, which exposes them to the fullest degree. I merely want to emphasize that by the side of Zinoviev, Kamenev, Evdokimov and Bakayev should stand Smirnov, Ter-Vaganyan and Mrachkovsky. They ought to stand side by side. Together they directed their criminal activities against our government, together they murdered Kirov and, therefore, together and fully must they answer for this.

Smirnov understands this perfectly well, and that is why he adopted a position of denial. At first he denied everything: he denied the existence of a Trotskyite organization, he denied the existence of a centre, he denied his participation in the centre, he denied connection with Trotsky, he denied that he gave any secret instructions, even those which he gave in 1936, and we know that this great conspirator managed to organize the communication of criminal instructions to his adherents even while he was isolated. He denied everything—he denied the existence of the Trotskyite centre in 1931, he denied the existence of such a centre in 1932. He denied everything. The whole of his examination of May 20 consisted solely of the words: "I deny that, again I deny, I deny." That is the only thing left for him to do.

Accused Smirnov, your experience, your skill in deceit, has betrayed you. Exposed by the evidence of Safonova, Mrachkovsky and Ter-Vaganyan, you were compelled to admit that there was a centre, that you were a member of this centre. Your denials were of no avail. You denied that you had received any instructions on terrorism, but you were exposed on this matter by Gaven, and you confessed; you were exposed by Holtzman who received instructions from Trotsky to be conveyed to you personally, and only to you, instructions to the effect that it was now necessary to adopt terrorism. Holtzman, whose Trotskyite allegiance was kept a particularly profound secret, said that he had received these instructions, but did not communicate them; and you think that this can be believed. No, no one will believe this.

Holtzman adopted the same position as Smirnov—I admit everything except terrorism—because he knows that for terrorism he may have to pay with his head. Smirnov was exposed as a terrorist by Holtzman, by Mrachkovsky, by Safonova and by Dreitzer.

On July 21, you, Smirnov, gave somewhat different evidence, that is to say, at first you denied that you had received any instructions from Trotsky to organize terrorism, but here you admitted that you did receive them. Your denials came to nought.

When confronted with Mrachkovsky, you continued to deny that you had received from Trotsky and conveyed to Mrachkovsky instructions to organize a terrorist group. Mrachkovsky put you to shame by saying: "Why, Ivan Nikitich, you want to get out of a sordid bloody business with a clean shirt?" I can repeat this: "Do you really think, accused Smirnov, that you will get out of this bloody business unscathed?" In reply to Mrachkovsky you said: "Invention and slander," but later you did confess' to something.

You admitted that the *bloc* was organized on the principle of the necessity of terrorism, and therefore you were one of the organizers of the terrorist centre. You received instructions on terror from Trotsky. On that basis you developed terroristic criminal activities. True, your arrest hindered you somewhat from taking part in the carrying out of these activities; nevertheless you did all you possibly could to help these activities.

I want to remind you that the confrontation with Safonova during the preliminary investigation, which, in the main reproduced what we saw in this Court, was very characteristic. Smirnov does not venture to deny Safonova's evidence. He invents an elastic form of lies. He knows that Safonova will not slander him, Safonova was formerly his wife, and has no personal grudge against him; therefore, he cannot plead a personal grudge. He says: "I do not remember," "evidently such a conversation may have taken place." He is asked: Was there any talk about organizing terrorism? He replies: "There was not, but there might have been." When now, masking himself, he says: "I have nothing to reply to that," he is guided by the same animal cowardice. But on August 13 he was compelled to admit that this conversation did take place in 1932, that he,

Smirnov, bears full responsibility for this, and that now he does not intend to evade responsibility.

I now want to deal with Ter-Vaganyan. He, too, at first, adopted a position of denial; but on August 14 he gave more truthful evidence. Summing up his testimony and his behaviour in Court we can draw several definite deductions: we may consider it established that Ter-Vaganyan was a member of the Trotskyite-Zinovievite centre, that he took an active part in organizing the centre, that he carried out the instructions of the centre on the basis of Trotsky's instructions which were received through Smirnov, and of which he learned from Smirnov. He tries to assert that actually he did nothing. But I must say beforehand that even if he "did nothing," what he did is sufficient to deserve the penalty provided for in Arts. 58^8, 19 and 58^8, 58^{1r} of the Criminal Code.

Moissei Lurye and Nathan Lurye. We have heard Nathan Lurye's evidence of how he arrived here and for what purpose, of the work he carried on in preparation for terroristic acts under the guidance of Moissei Lurye, of how, in fact, he was practically the successor to the group which had been gotten together here before him by Franz Weitz, the fascist agent and a trusted man of Himmler, chief of the fascist black secret service, chief of the German S. S. detachments and subsequently, chief of the German Gestapo.

You remember all their evidence, and I do not think it is necessary to deal with it in detail. It has been fully, categorically, and unquestionably proved that Nathan Lurye and Moissei Lurye prepared to commit terroristic acts. They must bear full responsibility for this crime!

When I spoke of the methods by which these gentlemen operated I showed, tried to show, to what depths these people had sunk, morally and politically. And perhaps one of the most striking and characteristic proofs of the depths of moral turpitude to which these people have sunk, of their lack of even those "moral" principles and rules of conduct by which even hardened criminals and gangsters are guided, is what Reingold told us about here. I refer to their plan to remove the traces of their foul crimes.

Was it an accident, comrades judges, that they, in expectation of successfully carrying out their heinous plan, intended to appoint none other than Bakayev as chairman of the O.G.P.U.— precisely Bakayev, who is known as a man filled with malicious hatred, as a resolute man, persevering and persistent, with a very strong will, strong character and stamina, who would not stop at anything to achieve the aims which he had set himself!

If some of the accused coolly planned to come to power over mountains of corpses of the best people of our Soviet land, then Bakayev was perhaps the most determined and most implacable executor of this plan! It is precisely this man that they intended to appoint as chairman of the O.G.P.U. in the event of their plot being successful.

I will not deal with the ludicrous distribution of portfolios among the conspirators and terrorists. I merely emphasize once again that none other than Bakayev was intended for the post of chairman of the O.G.P.U. Zinoviev and Kamenev did not exclude the possibility that the O.G.P.U. was in possession of the threads of the plot that they were hatching against the state, and, therefore, they considered it to be one of their most important tasks to appoint Bakayev chairman of the O.G.P.U. He was to obtain possession of all these threads and then destroy them, as well as the very people who carried out Zinoviev's and Kamenev's instructions.

Kamenev and Zinoviev do not deny the first part of this, but they deny the second part. That second part is too ghastly, and Zinoviev said it was taken from Jules Verne. But do we not know that there have been such examples in history? Do we not know certain neighbouring states in which such procedure has been applied, where participants in a plot were physically exterminated by the hand of the organizers of the plot, as was the case with Roehm and his henchmen?

Accused Zinoviev, you yourself say that it was intended to appoint Bakayev to the post of chairman of the O.G.P.U. in order to use him for the purpose of removing the traces of your crime. Why, then, do you say this is from Jules Verne? You have chosen a faulty line of defence.

This is not very important for the case; but that is not the question, that is not the point. This is one of the remarkable touches which characterize the people who aspired to the leadership of our country. It proves how fortunate we are that they were removed from this leadership in time!

Zinoviev and Kamenev call this fantastic tales from the Arabian Nights. But, by your leave, what about the murder of Zinoviev's secretary Bogdan? What is that? A tale? Zinoviev could not say anything about that; but Reingold revealed it and Pickel confirmed it.

Zinoviev recommended Bogdan to Bakayev as a suitable person to commit terroristic acts.

Reingold said it, Pickel confirmed it, but Bakayev vigorously denies it and tries to escape from it. But it is a fact which nobody can escape. Reingold and Pickel have proved that Bogdan's "suicide" was really murder. It was done by Bakayev on the instructions of the united centre! "You are hesitating to carry out the instructions of our united Trotskyite-Zinovievite centre? Kill yourself or else we will kill you." That is what Bakayev said to Bogdan, and Bogdan gave way.

This was the beginning of the execution of the plan drawn up by Zinoviev and Kamenev that was to be carried out in the event of the terroristic plot turning out successful. Zinoviev and Kamenev tried to depict Bogdan's suicide as the fate of a "victim" of our Soviet regime. But you yourselves drove Bogdan to suicide by confronting him with the dilemma: either to carry out a terroristic act or to commit suicide.

Comrades judges, if you link up this episode with all the methods of struggle, all the other methods of "work" adopted by this criminal gang, you will easily understand the truthfulness of the evidence given by Reingold and Pickel, who in this Court again and again exposed Zinoviev, Kamenev and Evdokimov as the perpetrators of a number of grave crimes.

Dogs Gone Mad Should All Be Shot

I now conclude, comrades judges. The last hour is approaching, the hour of reckoning for these people who have committed grave crimes against our great country. It is the last hour of reckoning for these people who took up arms against our dearest and most beloved, against the beloved leaders of our Party and our country, against Stalin, Kaganovich, Voroshilov, Orjonikidze, Zhdanov, Postyshev, Kossior and other leaders of our land of victorious, growing and flourishing, new, socialist society. A sad and shameful end awaits these people who were once in our ranks, although they were never distinguished for either staunchness or loyalty to the cause of socialism.

Just a few words more. Some of the accused tried to draw a parallel with the historical past, with the period of the Narodnaya Volya. They tried to compare some people with the heroic terrorists who in the last century entered into combat with the terrible, cunning and ruthlessly cruel enemy, the tsarist government. In speaking of Bakayev, or perhaps of Smirnov, the name of Gershuni was mentioned here. This argument does not hold water.

That was a struggle waged by a handful of self-sacrificing enthusiasts against the gendarme giant; it was a fight in the interests of the people. We Bolsheviks have always opposed terrorism, but we must pay our tribute to the sincerity and heroism of the members of the Narodnaya Volya. Gershuni was not a Bolshevik, but he, too, fought against tsarism and not against the people.

You, however, a handful of downright counter-revolutionaries, representatives of the vanguard of the international counter-revolution, you took up arms against the vanguard of the world proletarian revolution! You took up arms against the liberty and happiness of the peoples. The comparison with the period of Narodnaya Volya terrorism is shameless. Filled with respect for the memory of those who in the times of the Narodnaya Volya sincerely and honestly, although employing, it is true, their own special, but always irreproachable methods, fought against the tsarist autocracy for liberty—I emphatically reject this sacrilegious parallel. I repeat, this parallel is out of place here. Before us are criminals, dangerous, hardened, cruel and ruthless towards our people, towards our ideals, towards the leaders of our

163

struggle, the leaders of the land of Soviets, the leaders of the toilers of the whole world!

The enemy is cunning. A cunning enemy must not be spared. The whole people rose to its feet as soon as these ghastly crimes became known. The whole people is quivering with indignation and I, as the representative of the state prosecution, join my anger, the indignant voice of the state prosecutor, to the rumbling of the voices of millions!

I want to conclude by reminding you, comrades judges, of those demands which the law makes in cases of the gravest crimes against the state. I take the liberty of reminding you that it is your duty, once you find these people, all sixteen of them, guilty of crimes against the state, to apply to them in full measure those articles of the law which have been preferred against them by the prosecution.

I demand that dogs gone mad should be shot—every one of them!

AUGUST 22 (EVENING SESSION)

After the opening of the evening session the President of the Court Comrade Ulrich addresses each of the accused, granting them the floor for their speeches of defence, since they refused counsel of defence. All the accused in turn tell the Court that they will not make their speeches of defence, giving as the reason that they will avail themselves of their right of the last plea. A number of the accused emphasize that they do not regard themselves entitled to defence as they recognize the correctness of the charges made against them.

After a short recess the Court commences the hearing of the last pleas of the accused.

The first to speak is Mrachkovsky.

The accused Mrachkovsky starts his last plea by relating his autobiography. Then he goes on to say:

"In 1923 I became a Trotskyite. I took a despicable path, the path of deception of the Party. We must cross out past services; the past does not exist. But the present cannot be crossed out. I am a counter-revolutionary. . . .

"I do not ask for mitigation of my punishment," continues Mrachkovsky. "I do not want that. I want to be believed that during the investigation and in court I told the whole truth. I want to depart from life without carrying any filth with me.

"Why did I take the counter-revolutionary path?" says Mrachkovsky further. "My connection with Trotsky—that is what brought me to this; it is from that time on that I began to deceive the Party, to deceive its leaders. Some may say: 'The Party gave no help; it might have been possible perhaps to wrest the fellow from counter-revolution and save him, but the Party took no measures.' That would not be true. The Party did all it could to tear me away from counter-revolution. The Party helped me and helped me a great deal.

"I think I have said everything," says Mrachkovsky in conclusion. "Let everybody remember that not only a general, not only a prince or nobleman can become a counter-revolutionary; workers or those who spring from the working class, like myself, can also become counter-revolutionaries.

"I depart as a traitor to my Party, as a traitor who should be shot. All I ask is that I be believed when I say that during the investigation I spat out all this vomit."

*   *   *

"Who will believe a single word of ours?" asks Evdokimov in opening his last plea. "Who will believe us, who played so detestable a comedy at the fresh grave of Kirov whom we had killed; who will believe us, who only by accident, not through any fault of our own, did not become the assassins of Stalin and other leaders of the people? Who will believe us, who are facing the Court as a counter-revolutionary gang of bandits, as allies of fascism, of the Gestapo? Did the heart of even a single one of us, who were convicted in the last year's trial of the Zinovievites in Leningrad, shudder at the thought of our accomplices remaining at liberty, knowing as we did, although in prison, that any day, any hour, another dastardly shot may be fired? Not one of us did what he should have done had we been bound by the thinnest of threads to the cause of the revolution.

"The difference between us and the fascists is very much in our disfavour. Fascism openly and frankly inscribed on its banner: 'Death to Communism.' On our lips we had all the time 'Long Live Communism,' whereas by our deeds we were fighting socialism victorious in the U.S.S.R. In words—'Long live the Communist Party of the Soviet Union.' In deeds—preparation for the assassination of the members of the Political Bureau of the Central Committee of the Party, one of whom we did kill. In words—'Down with imperialism,' in deeds—banking on the defeat of the U.S.S.R. in the struggle against international imperialism."

Continuing, the accused Evdokimov says: "Trotsky is not with us here in the dock because he is abroad. He has two perspectives before him: either to disappear immediately and without a trace, as Azef did, not only from the political arena, but from the arena of life in general and go into oblivion, hide behind some false name as Azef did—or else, at some time, face a proletarian court."

"I don't consider it possible to plead for clemency," says Evdokimov in conclusion. "Our crimes against the proletarian state and against the international revolutionary movement are too great to make it possible for us to expect clemency."

*   *   *

"The political importance and the past of each of us," says Dreitzer, "were not the same. But, having become assassins, we have all become equals here. I, at any rate, am one of those who have no right to expect nor to ask for mercy."

*   *   *

"Whatever our fate may be," says the accused Reingold in his last plea, "we have been already shot politically. The representative of the State prosecution, speaking with the voice of 170,000,000 Soviet people, demanded that we be shot like mad dogs. I knew where I was going and what I was going for. I and the whole of the terrorist Trotskyite-Zinovievite organization sitting here have been exposed by this trial as the shock troop, as a white-guard, fascist shock troop, of the international counter-revolutionary bourgeoisie.

"The circle has closed. It is over with the political masquerade, it is over with the shams of oppositions, discussions and platforms. Opposition was superseded by conspiracy against the state; discussions and platforms were superseded by bullets and bombs." In conclusion Reingold says:

"Our trial, the trial of the Trotskyite-Zinovievite terrorist and fascist organization, will bury the political corpses of Zinoviev, Kamenev and Trotsky, and of his shadow, his loyal armour-bearer, Smirnov, as under a heavy tombstone.

"I fully admitted my guilt. It is not for me to plead for mercy."

*   *   *

"I am guilty of the assassination of Kirov," declares Bakayev. "I took a direct part in the preparation of other terroristic acts against the leaders of the Party and the government. I am prepared to bear full responsibility. We Trotskyites and Zinovievites

167

not only worked for the benefit of the international counter-revo-lutionary bourgeoisie, we also worked hand in hand with the agents of the most bitter enemy of the working class, fascism.

"The facts which were revealed before this Court show to the whole world that the organizer of this unprecedented Trotskyite-Zinovievite counter-revolutionary terrorist *bloc*, its moving spirit, is Trotsky. I have wagered my head over and over in the interests of Zinoviev and Kamenev. I am heavily oppressed by the thought that I became an obedient tool in the hands of Zinoviev and Kame-nev, became an agent of the counter-revolution, that I raised my hand against Stalin."

Bakayev turns to Zinoviev and accuses him of not being frank even at this trial.

Bakayev concludes by stating that he realizes the gravity of his crime and awaits the deserved and just verdict of the prole-tarian court.

*   *   *

The accused Pickel makes a detailed review of the history of the development of the Trotskyite-Zinovievite opposition which became a gang of counter-revolutionary terrorists. He says that from 1925 onwards, the struggle this opposition waged against the Party and its Central Committee contained all the elements of political banditry. The struggle started with filthy insinuations against the Party leadership and ended with terroristic acts.

"Only one conclusion can be drawn," says Pickel. "We repre-sent a most brutal gang of criminals who are nothing more nor less than a detachment of international fascism. Trotsky, Zinoviev and Kamenev were our banner. To this banner were drawn not only we, the dregs of the land of Soviets, but also spies, and agents of foreign states and those sent here for diversive activities.

"The last eight years of my life have been years of baseness, years of terrible, nightmarish deeds. I must bear my deserved punishment."

*   *   *

With this the evening session closes.

AUGUST 23 (MORNING SESSION)

During the morning session of August 23 the last pleas of the accused are continued.

"I, together with Zinoviev and Trotsky," declares Kamenev, "was the organizer and leader of a terrorist plot which planned and prepared a number of terroristic attempts on the lives of the leaders of the government and the Party of our country, and which carried out the assassination of Kirov.

"For ten years, if not more," continues Kamenev, "I waged a struggle against the Party, against the government of the land of Soviets, and against Stalin personally. In this struggle, it seems to me, I utilized every weapon in the political arsenal known to me —open political discussion, attempts to penetrate into factories and works, illegal leaflets, secret printing presses, deception of the Party, the organization of street demonstrations, conspiracy and, finally, terrorism.

"I once studied the history of the political movements and I cannot remember any form of political struggle that we did not use during the past ten years. The proletarian revolution allowed us a period of time for our political struggle which no other revolution gave its enemies. The bourgeois revolution of the 18th century gave its enemies weeks and days, and then destroyed them. The proletarian revolution gave us ten years in which to reform and to realize that we were in error. But we did not do that. Three times was I reinstated in the Party. I was recalled from exile merely on the strength of my personal statement. After all the mistakes I had committed I was entrusted with responsible missions and posts. This is the third time I am facing a proletarian court on the charge of terroristic intentions, designs and actions.

"Twice my life was spared. But there is a limit to everything, there is a limit to the magnanimity of the proletariat, and that limit we have reached. I ask myself," says Kamenev further, "is it an accident that alongside of myself, Zinoviev, Evdokimov, Bakayev and Mrachkovsky are sitting emissaries of foreign secret-police departments, people with false passports, with dubious biographies and undoubted connections with the Gestapo. No! It is not an accident. We are sitting here side by side with the agents of foreign secret-police departments because our weapons were the same, because our arms became intertwined before our fate became intertwined here in this dock.

"Thus," says Kamenev in conclusion, "we served fascism, thus we organized counter-revolution against socialism, prepared, paved the way for the interventionists. Such was the path we took, and such was the pit of contemptible treachery and all that is loathsome into which we have fallen.

*   *   *

"I want to say once again," says the accused Zinoviev at the outset of his last plea, "that I admit that I am fully and completely guilty. I am guilty of having been an organizer of the Trotskyite-Zinovievite *bloc* second only to Trotsky, the *bloc* which set itself the aim of assassinating Stalin, Voroshilov and a number of other leaders of the Party and the government. I plead guilty to having been the principal organizer of the assassination of Kirov.

"The Party," continues Zinoviev, "saw where we were going and warned us. In one of his speeches Stalin pointed out that tendencies may arise among the opposition to impose its will upon the Party by violence. At one of the conferences held before the XIV Congress of the Party, Dzerzhinski called us Kronstadtists. Stalin, Voroshilov, Orjonikidze, Dzerzhinski and Mikoyan did all they could to persuade us, to save us. Scores of times they said to us: you may do enormous harm to the Party and the Soviet government, and you yourselves will perish in doing so. But we did not heed these warnings. We entered into an alliance with Trotsky. We filled the place of the Mensheviks, Socialist-Revolutionaries and whiteguards who could not come out openly in our country. We took the place of the terrorism of the Socialist-Revolutionaries. Not the pre-revolutionary terrorism which was directed against the autocracy, but the Right Socialist

Revolutionaries' terrorism of the period of the Civil War, when the S-R's shot at Lenin.

"My defective Bolshevism became transformed into anti-Bolshevism, and through Trotskyism I arrived at fascism. Trotskyism is a variety of fascism, and Zinovievism is a variety of Trotskyism.

"Believe me, citizens judges, if I say that I suffered the greatest punishment, greater than anything that awaits me, when I heard the testimony of Nathan Lurye and the testimony of Olberg. I felt and understood that my name will be associated with the names of those who stood beside me. On my right hand Olberg, on my left—Nathan Lurye. . . ."

*　　*　　*

In his last plea Smirnov deals in detail with the history of his struggle against the Party leadership after he was forgiven by the Party and reinstated into its ranks in 1929.

"I returned to the Party," says Smirnov, "in 1929-30, and the Party did all it could to help me get on the right track. But I was unable to justify its confidence."

Continuing, Smirnov says that in 1931 he resumed the fight against the Party leadership.

"This was the mistake I made, which later grew into a crime. It induced me to resume contact with Trotsky, it induced me to seek connections with the Zinovievite group, it brought me into a *bloc* with the group of Zinovievites, into receiving instructions on terrorism from Trotsky through Gaven in November 1932, it brought me to terrorism. I communicated Trotsky's instructions on terrorism to the *bloc* to which I belonged as a member of the centre. The *bloc* accepted these instructions and began to act."

Then Smirnov continues, just as during the preliminary investigation and the trial, to deny responsibility for the crimes committed by the Trotskyite-Zinovievite terrorist centre after his arrest.

Further, Smirnov appeals to all his adherents resolutely to break with the past, to fight against Trotskyism and Trotsky. He declares: "There is no other path for our country but the one it is now treading, and there is not, nor can there be, any other leadership than that which history has given us. Trotsky, who sends directions and instructions on terrorism, and regards our

171

state as a fascist state, is an enemy; he is on the other side of the barricade; he must be fought."

*   *   *

"My entire political outlook," says Olberg, "took shape under the influence of Trotsky and Trotskyism. Following Trotsky, I shrank neither from terrorism nor from agreements with the fascists. The aims of the Trotskyite counter-revolutionary organization and the hopelessness of these aims became particularly clear to me at this trial during which I saw, quite distinctly, how pitiful were the leaders of the Trotskyite-Zinovievite counter-revolution who led us, the young ones, along the path of terroristic struggle, and how great was the power of the Soviet state... I ask the Supreme Court to give me the opportunity of trying at least to some extent to atone for my monstrous crimes."

*   *   *

"In my last plea," says Berman-Yurin, "I do not want to defend myself by any arguments. There are no such arguments. I repented, but too late. Yesterday, in his speech for the prosecution, the citizen State Prosecutor drew the complete picture of my crimes. And the proletarian state will deal with me as I deserve. It is too late for contrition."

*   *   *

"Here," says Holtzman, "in the dock beside me, is a gang of murderers, not only murderers, but fascist murderers. I do not ask for mercy."

*   *   *

"My crime is clear, it has been proved," says N. Lurye. "I do not know what I might still say in my defence. In my last plea I can only express regret for what I have done . . . but my regret comes too late."

*   *   *

In his last plea M. Lurye says:

"I did not conceal anything, I cannot be reproached for that. The State Prosecutor demanded that I be sternly punished. But can my crime be compared with the crime of my chief?"

M. Lurye pleads mitigating circumstances.

*   *   *

With this the morning session closes.

172

AUGUST 23 (EVENING SESSION)

During the evening session of August 23, last pleas are made by Ter-Vaganyan and Fritz David.

*   *   *

In his last plea, the accused Ter-Vaganyan fully admits his guilt before the Soviet state and the Party.

"I am crushed by the weight of all that was revealed here," says Ter-Vaganyan. "I am crushed by the speech of the State Prosecutor."

"It is very hard to bear when, by the whole course of one's crime, one finds oneself in the position of an enemy, of a fascist being tried by a proletarian court. In such a moment it would of course be hypocrisy if I did not say one thing: I would like to have the opportunity of exerting every effort to fill the abyss, the chasm, which separates me from my former comrades.

"I bow my head in guilt before the Court and say: whatever your decision may be, however stern your verdict, I accept it as deserved."

*   *   *

"I want to assure the proletarian Court," says the accused Fritz David, "that I curse Trotsky. I curse that man who ruined my life and pushed me into heinous crime."

*   *   *

At 7. p. m. the Court withdraws to the Council Chamber.

*   *   *

On August 24, at 2:30 p.m., the president, Comrade Ulrich, reads the verdict.

173

THE VERDICT

In the name of the Union of Soviet Socialist Republics
the Military Collegium of the Supreme Court of the U.S.S.R., consisting of:

President: the President of the Military Collegium of the Supreme Court of the U.S.S.R., Army Military Jurist, Comrade *V. V. Ulrich;*

Members: the Vice-Presidents of the Military Collegium of the Supreme Court of the U.S.S.R., Army Corps Military Jurist, Comrade *I. L. Matulevich,* and Divisional Military Jurist, Comrade *I. T. Nikitchenko;*

Secretary: Military Jurist of First Rank, Comrade *Kostyushko;*

State Prosecution being represented by the State Attorney of the U.S.S.R., Comrade *A. Y. Vyshinsky,*

in an open court session, in the city of Moscow, on August 19-24, 1936 heard the case against:

1. *Zinoviev,* Grigori Evseyevich, born 1883, employee, sentenced on January 16, 1935, in the Zinovievite "Moscow centre" case to imprisonment for ten years in accordance with Articles 17 and 58^8 of the Criminal Code of the R.S.F.S.R.;

2. *Kamenev,* Lev Borisovich, born 1883, employee, sentenced on January 16, 1935 in the Zinovievite "Moscow centre" case to imprisonment for five years, in accordance with Articles 17 and 58^8 of the Criminal Code of the R.S.F.S.R., and again sentenced on July 27, 1935, to imprisonment for ten years, in accordance with Articles 17 and 58^8 of the Criminal Code of the R.S.F.S.R.;

3. *Evdokimov,* Grigori Eremeyevich, born 1884, employee, sentenced on January 16, 1935, in the Zinovievite "Moscow centre" case to imprisonment for eight years in accordance with Articles 17 and 58^8 of the Criminal Code of the R.S.F.S.R.;

4. *Bakayev,* Ivan Petrovich, born 1887, employee, sentenced on January 16, 1935 in the Zinovievite "Moscow centre" case to imprisonment for eight years in accordance with Articles 17 and 58^8 of the Criminal Code of the R.S.F.S.R.;

5. *Mrachkovsky,* Sergei Vitalievich, born 1883, employee;

6. *Ter-Vaganyan,* Vagarshak Arutyunovich, born 1893, employee;

7. *Smirnov,* Ivan Nikitich, born 1880, employee

all seven being charged with having committed crimes covered by Articles 58^8 and 58^{11} of the Criminal Code of the R.S.F.S.R.

8. *Dreitzer,* Ephim Alexandrovich, born 1894, employee;

9. *Reingold,* Isak Isayevich, born 1897, employee;

10. *Pickel,* Richard Vitoldovich, born 1896, employee;

11. *Holtzman,* Edouard Solomonovich, born 1882, employee;

12. *Fritz David,* alias Kruglyansky, Ilya-David Israilevich, born 1897, employee;

13. *Olberg,* Valentine Pavlovich, born 1907, employee;

14. *Berman-Yurin,* Konon Borisovich, alias Alexander Fomich, born 1901, employee;

15. *Lurye,* Moissei Ilyich, alias Emel, Alexander, born 1897, employee;

16. *Lurye,* Nathan Lazarevich, born 1901, employee

all being charged with having committed crimes covered by Articles 19 and 58^8, 58^{11} of the Criminal Code of the R.S.F.S.R.

The preliminary and court investigations have established that:

In the autumn of 1932, on the instructions of L. Trotsky received by I. N. Smirnov, leader of the Trotskyite underground organization in the U.S.S.R., a union took place between the Trotskyite and Zinovievite underground counter-revolutionary groups which formed a "united centre" consisting of Zinoviev, Kamenev, Evdokimov and Bakayev (representing the Zinovievites), and of Smirnov, Ter-Vaganyan and Mrachkovsky (representing the Trotskyites).

The union of these counter-revolutionary groups was achieved on the basis of the use of individual terror against the leaders of the C.P.S.U. and the Soviet Government.

The Trotskyites and Zinovievites, on the direct instructions of Trotsky, received by the "united centre" through the accused Smirnov, Holtzman and Dreitzer, in this period (1932-36) concentrated all their hostile activities against the Soviet Government and the C.P.S.U. on the organization of terror against their leaders.

The Court has established that the "united centre," on the direct instructions of L. Trotsky and Zinoviev, organized and carried out on December 1, 1934, through the medium of the underground terrorist Leningrad Zinovievite group of Nikolayev-Kotolynov, the foul murder of the member of the Presidium of the Central Executive Committee of the U.S.S.R. and member of the Central Committee of the C.P.S.U., Comrade Sergei Mironovich Kirov.

Not confining themselves to the assassination of Comrade Kirov, the Trotskyite-Zinovievite centre prepared a number of terroristic acts against Comrades Stalin, Voroshilov, Zhdanov, L. M. Kaganovich, Orjonikidze, Kossior and Postyshev.

The materials of the court investigation and the confessions of the accused Zinoviev, Kamenev, Evdokimov, Bakayev, Mrachkovsky and Dreitzer have established that L. Trotsky, from abroad, and Zinoviev within the country, expedited by every means the preparations for the murder of Comrade S. M. Kirov. For the purpose of expediting the murder of Comrade S. M. Kirov, Kamenev, in June 1934, on the instructions of the united Trotskyite-Zinovievite centre went to Leningrad where he conducted negotiations with the leader of one of the Leningrad terrorist groups, Yakovlev, whose case has been set aside for a separate trial, about the organization of this terroristic act against Comrade Kirov.

The Court has also established that on the instructions of the "united centre" the accused Bakayev, in November 1934, also made a special journey to Leningrad to check up on the preparedness of the Leningrad terrorist group of Nikolayev-Kotolynov for the carrying out of the assassination of Comrade Kirov. At a secret meeting of the members of this Leningrad terrorist group, Bakayev heard the report of Leonid Nikolayev, the murderer of Comrade Kirov, and, in the name of the united Trotskyite-Zinovievite centre, gave him and his accomplices a number of practical instructions concerning the organization of the assassination of Comrade S. M Kirov. It was in conformity with these instructions that L. Nikolayev and his accomplices committed the foul murder of Comrade S. M. Kirov on December 1, 1934.

The Court has also established that in 1934, the accused Bakayev, Reingold and Dreitzer, in accordance with the decisions of the "united centre," twice tried to make an attempt on the life of Comrade Stalin.

In order the more successfully to commit the terroristic acts planned by the "united centre" it organized in 1933 in the city of Moscow, the so-called "Moscow terrorist centre," consisting of the

176

accused Reingold, Pickel and Dreitzer, under the direct guidance of the accused Bakayev, a member of the "united centre."

The "united centre" instructed the accused Bakayev to make practical preparations for the assassination of Comrades Stalin and Kirov, and it instructed Dreitzer, a member of the "Moscow terrorist centre" to organize a terroristic act against Comrade Voroshilov.

Not confining himself to the organization of a number of terroristic acts against the leaders of the Soviet Government and the C.P.S.U. under the immediate direction of the "united centre," L. Trotsky, in the period of 1932-36, was systematically sending a number of terrorists into the U.S.S.R. from abroad for the same purpose.

In November 1932, L. Trotsky sent to the U.S.S.R. Berman-Yurin and Fritz David; and before leaving, the latter received from L. Trotsky personal instructions with regard to the organization of the assassination of Comrade Stalin.

In the same year, 1932, L. Trotsky sent to Moscow from Berlin the terrorist Nathan Lurye. In conjunction with Franz Weitz, agent of the Gestapo and a person trusted by Himmler, now chief of the Gestapo (Franz Weitz was then living in Moscow under the guise of a foreign specialist), Nathan Lurye made preparations for attempts on the lives of Comrades Stalin, Voroshilov, Kaganovich and Orjonikidze.

In the winter of 1932-33, after the departure of Franz Weitz from Moscow, Nathan Lurye and his terrorist group continued the preparation of these terroristic acts jointly with the accused Moissei Lurye who arrived in Moscow from Berlin in 1933, and who had also received from Trotsky instructions to expedite terroristic acts against the leaders of the Soviet Government and the C.P.S.U.

In 1934, while at Chelyabstroi, Nathan Lurye tried to make an attempt on the lives of Comrades Kaganovich and Orjonikidze. Finally, the said Nathan Lurye, on May 1, 1936, on the instruction of, and by previous agreement with, Moissei Lurye, tried to make an attempt on the life of Comrade Zhdanov during the First of May demonstration in Leningrad.

In the summer of 1935, L. Trotsky, through his son L. Sedov, sent to the U.S.S.R. from Berlin the terrorist V. Olberg, who used a false passport issued in the name of a subject of the Republic of Honduras. V. Olberg obtained this passport with the aid of the German secret police, the Gestapo, having first received the consent of L. Trotsky, through the latter's son, Sedov, to utilize the assistance of the German secret police in this matter.

On arriving in the U.S.S.R., V. Olberg established contact with the counter-revolutionary Trotskyite terrorist group in the city of Gorki, and trained a number of terrorists who were to commit a terroristic act against the leaders of the Soviet Government and the C.P.S.U. in the Red Square in Moscow on May 1, 1936.

The court investigation has also established that simultaneously with the preparation of terroristic acts against Comrades Stalin, Voroshilov, Zhdanov, Kaganovich and Orjonikidze, the Trotskyite-Zinovievite terrorist centre made preparations for terroristic acts against Comrades Kossior and Postyshev through the medium of the Ukrainian terrorist group operating under the direction of the Trotskyite Mukhin, whose case has been set aside for separate trial.

Thus it is established that

1) *G. E. Zinoviev;*
2) *L. B. Kamenev;*
3) *G. E. Evdokimov;*
4) *I. P. Bakayev;*
5) *S. V. Mrachkovsky;*
6) *V. A. Ter-Vaganyan* and
7) *I. N. Smirnov*

are guilty of:

a) Having organized the united Trotskyite-Zinovievite terrorist centre for the purpose of assassinating the leaders of the Soviet Government and of the C.P.S.U.,

b) Having prepared, and on December 1, 1934, perpetrated the foul murder of Comrade S. M. Kirov through the medium of the Leningrad underground terrorist group of Nikolayev-Kotolynov and others sentenced on December 29, 1934, by the Military Collegium of the Supreme Court of the U.S.S.R.,

c) Having organized a number of terrorist groups who made

178

preparations to assassinate Comrades Stalin, Voroshilov, Zhdanov, Kaganovich, Orjonikidze, Kossior and Postyshev—*i.e.*, crimes covered by Articles 58^8 and 58^{11} of the Criminal Code of the R.S.F.S.R.

8) *E. A. Dreitzer;*
9) *I. I. Reingold;*
10) *R. V. Pickel;*
11) *E. S. Holtzman;*
12) *Fritz David* (Kruglyansky, Ilya-David Israilevich) ;
13) *V. P. Olberg;*
14) *K. B. Berman-Yurin;*
15) *M. I. Lurye* (Emel, Alexander) and
16) *N. L. Lurye*

are guilty of having been, while members of the underground counter-revolutionary terrorist Trotskyite-Zinovievite organization, active participants in the preparations for the assassination of the leaders of the Party and the Government, Comrades Stalin, Voroshilov, Zhdanov, Kaganovich, Orjonikidze, Kossior and Postyshev,

i.e., crimes covered by Articles 19 and 58^8, 58^{11} of the Criminal Code of the R.S.F.S.R.

On the basis of the above, and guided by Articles 319 and 320 of the Code of Criminal Procedure of the R.S.F.S.R., the Military Collegium of the Supreme Court of the U.S.S.R.

Sentences:

1) *Zinoviev,* Grigori Evseyevich
2) *Kamenev,* Lev Borisovich
3) *Evdokimov,* Grigori Eremeyevich
4) *Bakayev,* Ivan Petrovich
5) *Mrachkovsky,* Sergei Vitalevich
6) *Ter-Vaganyan,* Vagarshak Arutyunovich
7) *Smirnov,* Ivan Nikitich
8) *Dreitzer,* Ephim Alexandrovich
9) *Reingold,* Isak Isayevich
10) *Pickel,* Richard Vitoldovich
11) *Holtzman,* Edouard Solomonovich
12) *Fritz David* (Kruglyansky, Ilya-David Israilevich)
13) *Olberg,* Valentine Pavlovich

14) *Berman-Yurın*, Konon Borisovich
15) *Lurye*, Moissei Ilyich (Emel, Alexander) and
16) *Lurye*, Nathan Lazarevich

all to the supreme penalty—to be shot, and all property personally belonging to them to be confiscated.

Lev Davidovich Trotsky, and his son, Lev Lvovich Sedov, now abroad, convicted by the evidence of the accused I. N. Smirnov, E. S. Holtzman, Dreitzer, V. Olberg, Fritz David (I. I. Kruglyansky) and Berman-Yurin, and also by the materials in the present case as having directly prepared and personally directed the organization in the U.S.S.R. of terroristic acts against the leaders of the C.P.S.U. and the Soviet State, are subject, in the event of their being discovered on the territory of the U.S.S.R., to immediate arrest and trial by the Military Collegium of the Supreme Court of the U.S.S.R.

Presiding:
[*Signed*]

V. V. ULRICH
President of the Military Collegium of the Supreme Court of the U.S.S.R.
Army Military Jurist

Members of the Court:
[*Signed*]

I. MATULEVICH
Vice-President of the Military Collegium of the Supreme Court of the U.S.S.R.
Army Corps Military Jurist

I. NIKITCHENKO
Vice-President of the Military Collegium of the Supreme Court of the U.S.S.R.
Divisional Military Jurist